9 Critical Elements To Enhance the Value of Your Clinic
The No-Nonsense Guide For Ophthalmologists to Get More Patients Utilizing The Internet

By Glenn J. Fournier

I0483891

Fournier Marketing
695 Evergreen Street, Greenfield, Tennessee 38230
gfournier@bellsouth.net
(731) 332-2350

There is no guarantee you will duplicate any of the results stated here. You recognize any business endeavor has inherent risk for loss of capital.

"The typical result one can expect to achieve is nothing. The "typical" person never gets to the end of this book. The "typical" person fails to implement anything. Thus they earn nothing. Zero. No income. And perhaps a loss of income. That's because "typical" people do nothing and therefore they achieve nothing. Be atypical. Do something. Implement something. If it doesn't work; make a change…and implement that. Try again…try harder. Persist. And reap the rewards."

Foreword

Glenn J. Fournier's "9 Critical Elements To Enhance the Value of Your Clinic" is an important book for any Ophthalmologist to read. Those of us who are veterans of Internet marketing know successful online business promotion never happens just by building a site and hoping customers will find it. Developing a successful website for your business is not rocket science – but expertise does involve a pretty steep learning curve. That's why I like this book so much. It gives an Ophthalmologist intelligent overview of what it takes to thrive online.

This book presents local online marketing in a way that even the most tech-adverse clinic owner can get an understanding of what they need to do next. It highlights some of the challenges in today's marketing world, and gives practical advice on overcoming them. It shows clinics how to connect better, faster, and easier with their prospective patients using the Internet.

In these pages you'll find hope – hope that your clinic can thrive even today, hope that you might be able to get back to whatever it was that attracted you to your field in the first place rather than working all the time to try to get new patients. Most importantly it provides a process for helping you connect with the people who really need the products and services your clinic offers.

Glenn explains local Internet marketing in a simple, conversational style that makes for an easy read. That's not to say any of this complicated strategy was over-simplified.

Anyone wanting to double or triple the value of their clinic should read and re-read this book. It can literally turn a dying clinic into one that's booming again. Around my company's headquarters, we often say we're in the business of creating heroes. Thanks, Glenn. Through your book, you're making a difference.

Mike Koenigs

Table of Contents

Introduction

A book about the Internet? At first, it didn't make sense. The Internet changes every day…and once it's printed, the book will be around forever. Then, we realized that while the Internet is fluid, and things do change from time to time, there are tried and true principles that will never change. In fact, they will only increase in effectiveness as the Internet grows and traditional advertising fades away. That is not to say traditional advertising is a lost cause.

This book has the best of both worlds.

What you find inside are the stable principles. In other words, they work…when implemented. They are based on the rock-solid strategies that we have been using with our clients for years. The results speak for themselves.

Of course, there are elements that change from time to time, and when we came across one of those, we analyze and decide if they are applicable to our clients for the best results.

I am going to use clinic/s, versus practice/s or business for conversational sake.

On that note, the difference between the average clinic and great clinics comes down to implementation. One often differs from another only in their willingness to implement the things they learn. The same is true for the information in this book. It works, and similar to everything you learned in school, it only works when implemented.

You knowing all of this information won't help you make any more money or sell your services or even your clinic for more. When you implement it, this information can make you an additional six figures or more in a year, PLUS you will help more people, create a more stable business, and gain some bragging rights at the next conference you attend.

Use it…and send us your success story.

One of the most common questions we get from Clinics is, "How am I supposed to get all of this done?"

The answer is that smart Doctors know how to build (or find) good teams. On that note, toward the end of the book, we have included a section on where and how to find competent people to help you implement your web strategy.

So, let's get started.

Chapter 1: **Patients For Life: How To Use The Internet To Fuel Your Local Practice/Clinic**

Congratulations! Just by getting to this first chapter, you're already ahead of your competition.

Why? Well, most people don't take the necessary action for success. You've gotten this far, now let's go the rest of the way together. At least you're forward-thinking. You know that the Internet is a big deal, and you know that your clinic is humming along very well; you might use the Internet to drum up a little business here and there, if you can, and maybe this book can help you supplement what you may be doing now.

You may think that the Internet won't help you all that much. People know you, you're in the Yellow Pages, in print ads and perhaps even TV ads and you're still getting a healthy amount of business.

Who searches for a local Ophthalmologist on the Internet, anyway?

The majority of your potential patients, that's who.

It is estimated that by 2017, 50% of the population will be Boomers!

Recent research shows that, increasingly, fulfillment of online searches is done overwhelmingly for local businesses. A study by BIA/Kelsey and research firm ComStat found that a staggering 97% of consumers research their purchases and local services online before they fulfill them at a local business. This isn't just the case with local services, either; major e-retailers are being beaten out by people who research products online but choose to buy them at local stores. This seems to speak to the fact that people like human interaction; they inform themselves online, but in the end they want that personal connection.

The consequence of this is that, unfortunately, any Clinic with no (or substandard) Internet presence is left out of that research process.

People want to fulfill their online searches locally, but if you don't pop up when they're doing their research, you'll simply fly under their radar and lose their business to another Clinic who has that Internet presence.

This is, of course, potentially very dangerous for any local Ophthalmology Clinic owner who has thus far avoided being on the Internet (or whose website is not producing results). It may sound alarmist or like nonsense, but it's true: the majority of potential patients are looking for their physician on the Internet, even preferring it over more traditional media like the Yellow Pages or TV. In fact, a study by comScore and TMP Directional Marketing showed that, for the first time, the number of patients searching for a local Ophthalmologist on the Internet exceeded that of the Yellow Pages, and Yellow Pages has headed downhill ever since. The fact of the matter is that people simply don't use the Yellow Pages anymore, since the Internet is a much easier and more convenient way to get information. The Yellow Pages has seen the light and now offers their online version called YP.

It's surprising at first, but it begins to make sense once you think about it. You can even look to your own habits as proof of this changing trend; how often do you use the Yellow Pages to find something you're looking for? Do you run over to your desk and flip through the Yellow Pages to find what you need, or do you do a quick Google search and find what you need right away? Even if you're still a Yellow Page user, take a look at others; your kids, friends, and family. How many of them use the Yellow Pages? If you're honest with yourself, it won't be surprising at all that the way people look for services has changed.

What is surprising is how many Ophthalmologists still have huge portions of their budget devoted to the Yellow Pages, TV and print ads. These options can still be viable if done properly.

Many Clinics can have $10,000 or more allocated to their Yellow Page advertising budget, which is, in this day and age, is simply a waste of money; Yellow Pages simply just aren't returning enough business to justify that sort of major investments. Of Clinics that can or do track ROI from print advertising campaigns, virtually all of them have seen diminishing returns. Every month, without fail, more people are using Google and other search engines instead of traditional media and methods of research; this isn't just a passing trend. Search has supplanted the Yellow Pages, and it's here to stay! An effective online presence isn't just a temporary strategy—it's forward-looking towards a future that has search engines as the main tool patients use to make their decisions.

SECTION BREAK: What that means for you

So how do you get in on this search corner of the market? After all, don't big Ophthalmology advertisers (i.e. LasikPlus) dominate search engine rankings on the Internet? Can local Clinics even compete in this ferocious online arena?

As it turns out, they can. Google has made some of the most significant changes to their search algorithm that we've seen in a long time; specifically, they've shifted searches for brick & mortar clinics to something called "local search return" or specifically Google Places / Google + Local, a feature that used to be only available on their Google Maps service.

What is local search return? Originally, when a user searched on Google Maps, local clinics would pop up in the area the user was searching for. If a user searched "Memphis, TN", for example, the Google interactive map that would appear also had helpful markers placed around the map, indicating local Eye Care Clinics that were nearby. Restaurants and hotels were the first businesses to jump on this feature and utilize it, and it was a natural fit; visitors to a new city need to know places to eat and sleep, and the Google Maps local search return feature was very useful to both users and service businesses by showing users where these local establishments were and facilitating that offline conversion.

Very soon, however, businesses besides restaurants and hotels realized that this service could benefit them greatly, and began listing themselves on the local search return maps as well. Eventually, Google realized that if users were searching maps to get this kind of information, then probably many of them are also searching in the regular search text box as well, not realizing that they had to go to the maps section to get those local search results. Again, look at your own search habits; how often do you go to Google Maps to search for something? Most likely, you simply type it into the google.com search box and hit enter.

Now, at this point in time, Google's regular search box was just returning lists of links as search results; they weren't map-based and often weren't nearly as useful as the map results that Google Maps was returning. As a result, Google started incorporating the local search returns into their regular search page. When you search for an Eye Care Clinic now on Google, it returns a map as well, with up to seven marked locations on the map that are all local Clinics. This is great news for local Ophthalmologists, because now there's a real chance for competition: a year ago, or even six months ago, local clinics simply couldn't compete on a national level with giants like Amazon or Wikipedia. Now, however, there's a very real chance for your Clinic to show up in the top three results on a local search page, a chance that will undoubtedly boost your online conversion, and a chance that wasn't there even a year ago.

Before, you had no chance of competing in any search; now, local Clinics have a chance to come out on top for local searches in their area. True, it's not easy; there are plenty of other clinics vying for these same spots, and just having a website up and some keywords isn't going to get you anywhere (and in fact, doing this process poorly can ensure that you never see the front page of Google at all). There is a process, however, and if you do a good job, are careful, and follow all the instructions in this book you'll have a very good shot at hitting the A, B, or C spots on your local search return!

WARNING

We mentioned that Google has changed its search algorithm- one of those changes involves duplicate content, which is now more dangerous than ever! There is one exception; it has to do with blog posts. Google has said many times, both verbally and in print, which it is striving to reward the real local business that has quality and substance to offer to their community. As a result, they are cracking down very harshly on anyone who's trying to game the system with shady methods such as duplicate content or fake listings; such actions will get you delisted from Google's search index entirely, and possibly for good. Though this may seem harsh or unreasonable, remember that Google's efforts to clean up its search engine only benefits you; you want them to go after the scammers and spammers so that you, a real clinic who can offer value and quality to consumers, can rise to the top to people who are genuinely looking for help and services.

In a similar vein, be very, very wary of companies who tell you this process is easy! It's not. They'll tell you it's just a matter of keywords, and to buy content and put it on multiple sites and your own. The problem is, much of this content is almost always rehashed, rewritten, or outright duplicated content, and you'll get next to no credit with Google at best, and delisted at worst. It also cuts two ways, because not only are you not gaining any ground, you're actually losing ground because Google's penalizing you. It's definitely not the way to go, and you'll be falling behind your competitors if you try and take this easy way out.

Quality, fresh, original content has always been the centerpiece for being successful online, and that doesn't show any signs of changing. Creating quality content doesn't have to be hard, but it does take time, patience, and discipline: there's a process to follow to ensure that you have the right kind of quality content that will get you ranked sky-high on Google! When it comes to content for Google, it doesn't just have to be the written word. Google now owns YouTube! Videos are a very powerful way to distribute your content and get your message out there. People have been trying to game the system with duplicate content and link farms for years, but Google has caught on to this sort of trickery and it's rapidly disappearing from the search engine landscape. Google removed over 48,000 websites recently for just this reason. Make sure not to get scammed by any of these offers – you know that if it seems too easy or cheap to be true- odds are that it probably is! Ask them if their content is duplicated, rewritten, or appears anywhere else; if they hem and haw before answering, run for the hills and don't look back!

With this book, you've received the system and process you need that will, with some time, effort, patience, and planning, get you to the top of the search results for your area!

JUST THE FACTS:

- The Internet is no longer optional. More and more, people are using it to find Ophthalmologists: You need to leverage it!

- Search is the big player now in Internet marketing. You need to make sure your page ranks high in the list of results when users search!

- Be very careful of how you enter the search engine market! A substandard presence online can be worse than no presence at all!

- If you need help, make sure to choose your marketers carefully! Some may attempt underhanded tricks to boost you in the search rankings (like duplicate content) but these tricks can often carry with them severe penalty from the search engines for trying to game the system!

Chapter 2: **Pretty Websites Can Kill Your Clinic: How to Get New Patients the RIGHT Way Online.**

So now we know how important Google is; we've taken a look at how recent changes have made local search return, and Google ranking in general, extremely important to your marketing efforts. We know that traditional media is fading fast, and if you want to stay on top of the game you're going to have to get into this search business straight away!

The natural next step would be to go and get ranked, and for that you need a website. Your website is as much a part of this process as anything else, and if you're going to get good conversions from your search rankings you need a functional website that fully caters to both the needs of your Clinic and the needs of your patients.

The creation of the website can be a minefield, especially in today's whiz-bang, Flash-enabled, Web 2.0 world where everyone thinks every website needs interactive menus, drop-down interfaces, and all other sorts of bells and whistles. You see it all the time, in fact, people ask for "Web 2.0" or "interactive" developers, or developers will try to push Flash this or Web 2.0 that on you, saying how important it is and how professional it makes your site look. You may be tempted to believe them.

In most cases web developers are using templates called WordPress Themes. These templates are difficult to optimize properly and more importantly they are not device responsive! What does that mean: the website can't be seen or read properly on tablets or Smartphone's.

The truth, however, is this: for most Clinics and conversion rates, all of that fancy stuff does not matter. A solid, simple website will work far better at increasing your conversion and getting patients to contact you. This may seem counter-intuitive, especially in a world that seems to value style over substance, but it's true: simpler pages have, both in our experience and in the experience of others, been far more effective at getting patients to call or email you than other, fancier, flashier pages.

This will seem a little daunting, especially considering how much we've been talking about the importance of getting listed properly. And that still holds true: getting ranked high on Google still matters the most. In fact, the rest of the book after this chapter is devoted to that very concept. The website, however, is an integral part of the chain. It's by no means the most important link in the chain, not by far; it needs to be done well, however, or it has the potential to ruin the entire concept of getting ranked on Google.

The bottom line is this: if your patient doesn't actually pick up the phone and call, all that effort you put in into getting visitors to your site will have been wasted. No matter how flashy, how fancy, how up-to-date your website is, if there are no conversions, then that website is not working for you, plain and simple!

SECTION BREAK: So What Does A Good Website Look Like?

It's a good question: if the flashy, stylish websites aren't for you, what is? What is the secret to getting visitors to pick up the phone and call?

Well, there are a few things. Let's take a look at them and find out how to build the website that will get the most visitors to pick up that phone and call your office!

Site Construction: What Should Your Overall Site Look Like?
In general, there is a rule that can be applied to websites looking to garner conversions from local search return: The less fancy the website is, the more conversions you'll get from it. Solid, functional sites will be far more effective for you. Keeping in that mentality, here is a general outline of what a sample website layout might look like:

- Home page
- Blog
- About Us / Services
- Contact Us (with map and phone)

And that's it.

It might seem a bit underwhelming to you, and vastly smaller than the majority of the websites you've visited, and you're right: those websites, however, are not ours. Your website is lean and mean, built for one purpose and one purpose only—to get people who go to your website to call you or email you. Anything else is a waste; it's nice that people come to visit your site, but that doesn't mean anything if nobody calls or if you don't capture someone's phone or email for future follow up.

Every page should also include a call to action (CTA). A call to action is something to get visitors to call you or email you right away. We'll talk more about the call to action later in the follow-up section, but just know that for local clinic websites we recommend, at a minimum, you include a banner or header that appears on every page; make sure your phone number appears in the top-right hand side or middle-right hand side.

Studies show, and our experience confirms, that people's eyes gravitate toward the right side of a page -- hint, look where Google puts their ads in their own search results. For added kick, add a form beneath the top phone number to sign up for your newsletter or to provide an incentive for people to provide their phone number and email address.

This is, of course, just an example; you are free to modify this layout however you wish. Depending on your Clinic, you may want to add a page about upcoming events you are hosting, or recent news and press about your Clinic. Know, however, that this basic layout works extremely well, and always, always remember: the less fancy the page, the better the results!

WARNING:
Please do not confuse less-fancy with bad design. You still want your business and website to look professional and we advocate a clean simple design. In fact we strongly feel that having less 'flashiness' to a website often leads to better visual design as there is less clutter, and better visual design also helps with conversions.

Your Clinic may already have invested in working with a branding agency to help create a logo and a set of colors that represent your "brand", carry those into your website. There are a number of color palette tools online where you can enter your Clinics core colors and they will provide you with suggested, visually appealing, complementary colors, for example Colour Lovers (http://www.colourlovers.com) or Color Combos (http://www.colorcombos.com). Look, you are a valuable professional in your community and your services are not (and should not be) cheap – don't make your website give potential patients the wrong impression.

This means you may not want to do it yourself and that you should be careful hiring your sister's friend's 22-year-old kid that calls himself a webmaster, but lives in his parents' basement.

Now, let's break down each of these pages more in-depth!

Home Page
There's not too much individuality going on here, but it's important for this page to connect your reader with the rest of the site. Make sure the page is easy on the eyes, has a blurb about you, and invites the reader to explore more of the site. Above all, however, make absolutely sure that the home page features the blog prominently!

This is so important, I'm going to give it its own line: Make sure the home page features the blog prominently. There are many ways to do this, some Clinics have the actual blog on the homepage; if you don't want to do this, think very, very carefully about how to prominently integrate your blog with the home page.

Video can be another important component for the homepage. Studies have shown a 30% increase in conversions when a visitor can watch a video of someone from the Clinic on the homepage. Yes, that is 30%. Incorporate a small, short (90 seconds – 2 minutes) video somewhere on your home page.

If you have any copy on your home page make it about no more than 3 things:

1.   The benefits you provide someone (not your services or 'features') but the actual benefits patients achieve as a result of working with you

2.   Information about what is on your blog and links / enticements to good blog posts

3.   Call to action – what can you provide in exchange for them to call or provide you their email or phone number. Special offers, special reports, checklists, etc.

These 3 items are so important to the success of a website that we actually write these sections for our private Clients and place them word-for-word.

Blog
Don't underestimate the blog, it's one of the most vital (if not the most vital) part of your website! It provides two things that are critical to your online success.

First, it is the home to new and relevant content to your prospects and patients.

You can talk about a lot of things that will be 'relevant' to your prospects and patients.

Obviously, you can discuss interesting things happening that affect your readers within your particular areas of expertise; talk about symptoms, advanced tools and techniques of eye care, etc.

You can also link out to a few recent news articles and provide some commentary about how they affect your readers.

A hidden gem of relevant content that most businesses overlook is to talk about local information. It doesn't have to pertain at all. You are a member of a community and if there is a sporting event, 5k, festival, or parade coming up, then write a few paragraphs about that and include links to all the details in one place. If you know that parking is tough on Saturdays around the area, provide information about other parking options; if there's a booth at the festival not to be missed, then tell your readers about that. You will be surprised that these will become your most popular blog posts. It also builds up your credibility as someone who lives, works, and cares about your community.

The second thing a blog provides is a place for the search engines to find new and relevant content about what your Clinic does and where it provides those services.

Everything we discussed above helps accomplish that, and by talking about your specific eye care profession you will naturally use the keywords that the search engines will pick up. Furthermore, talking about things going on in the local community will help the search engines understand the community, town, cities you should be associated with in the search results.

We hope that was simple to understand; very often, many marketing agencies make this part more complicated than it has to be. They talk about keywords, keyword density, latent search algorithms, and more. It doesn't have to be that hard! Write about stuff that you know about and that provide value to your readers: the two most obvious are your area and events going on in your community and nearby communities. If you hear someone talk about keyword density, just run away: it's our humble opinion that they're just trying to make it sound too complicated so they can charge more.

That's how important blogging is to us!

About Us

The About Us page is, oddly enough, one that many clinics get wrong. They're all too content just to throw up a little blurb about themselves, perhaps a map or two on how to get to them. This isn't enough info on you, and nor is it helping you drive conversions.

People care about your years of experience as a Ophthalmologist, sure, but that's not what's going to get them to call- it doesn't truly distinguish you from the other Ophthalmologists in the pack, or give them a reason to give you their business. You have to think instead about something called a unique selling position- why do patients like to work with you and continue working with you? Information about you, your clinic, why you're different, etc. and so forth just doesn't cut it—you have to show them why you're ahead of the pack, and ultimately show them why they, as a consumer, want to work with you and not the other clinics in the area.

Think about it this way: most people care about one thing and one thing only. WIIFM.

That stands for "What's In It For Me."

Your prospects could honestly care less about your degrees, titles, or positions. Sorry. What they really want to know is if you can solve their problem, and solve it fast and professionally.

So instead of talking about you, talk about them and what they will benefit from working with you.

That one tip alone, in fact, will set your website above and beyond most of the Ophthalmologists we see and even some we work with: they simply don't set themselves apart sufficiently, and by doing so you'll gain a very competitive edge in this field.

Contact Us

The Contact Us page should be very simple. You should have your email, your phone number, and a map to your business. That's it. You can perhaps put a slightly different or stronger call to action on this page, but for the most part this page should be clean, simple, and have nothing to distract the reader from picking up the phone or putting in their email. Some people add a contact form on this page. That's perfectly fine to do, but the most important thing is to provide a clear phone number or email that is directed and answered by an actual human.

SECTION BREAK: Call To Action

So you've got the basic layout of your page all down. Just one thing left: your call to action.

So what makes an effective call to action, and how can you put that to use on your site to generate those conversions?

An effective call to action is one that makes the potential patient to pick up the phone and call right away, or give you their email. It's crucial that your call to action is very strong, because you're asking for information that's become more and more private in modern times. People know about spam, they know about scams, and they're hesitant to give out their email to just any site they find on the Internet. You have to overcome that initial hesitation and get them to give you their email. One way is to offer a special for providing information or calling now – like a big discount on a service. However, we've found that the way that works best is to provide a special report about something that will be very helpful to the consumer who found you by searching for an Ophthalmologist or whatever your Clinics' specialty is in your area.

Examples of this could be "Special Report: 3 critical things you need to know before ever hiring or calling an Ophthalmologist", "5 Frequently asked questions you need to know about your eye health", or "3 myths you've been led to believe about cataracts". It's important that these examples be specific to your practice; the more targeted your examples, the more likely it is that you're going to get someone to sign up who's interested in your area of expertise.

You can even make it more targeted by making it local, for example "3 things you need to know before hiring an Ophthalmologist in Little Rock, Arkansas". These examples could be strong enough to get someone to put in their email; they might say, "Hey, wow, what are those three things? I was ready to get moving and hire an Ophthalmologist tomorrow, but I better know this before I do anything" and then pop in their email and now you can quickly follow up with them (and even automate some of the follow-up).

This content is so important, that for our private Clients, we write this report for them and place it on their website (after their review, of course). The titles above take a "consumer advocacy" approach, which we've found gets a lot more patients than much of the traditional forms of advertising.

We also typically recommend that you not just ask for their email, but for their cell phone number as well. People are giving out their cell phone numbers quite readily now, more so than a few years ago, where it was very difficult to get someone's mobile number. Many people nowadays use cell phones as their primary or even only phone number, and thus they're more willing to give it out to people who ask if the reason is compelling enough.

If you follow all these steps, anyone who signs up with their email or phone number will be a "warm" lead. A "warm" lead is someone who's going to be very receptive to your Clinic and much easier to convert into a patient, since they've showed a great deal of interest in your services—they've pretty much done the hard part, which is getting in contact. You have to act on this, however; warm leads, like anything else warm, tend to cool over time, and if you don't act quickly it'll be that much harder to seal the deal. This leads us to our next item of interest: follow-up systems!

It's important that you have some sort of follow-up system in place so that you can call a lead within five minutes of them entering a form. It's vital that you have a stable, reliable follow-up system in place! If you can get them within 5 minutes, for example, you know they're an extremely warm lead; you know they were on the website, you know they were interested, and you know they're looking for business. This is a very warm lead, and much more so than someone who just happened to see your name in a direct mail piece or in a local flyer!

There are some automated follow-up systems in place that are used by many businesses; tools like with Constant Contact, Infusionsoft, among others. Depending on your area of expertise there are some services that even provide dozens of pre-written email templates that have proven to help convert email prospects into patients.

If you want to use something like these, that's perfectly fine, but make sure to put the call to action form on that all-important right-hand side first.

We'll talk more about follow-up later, in its own in-depth, complete section. First, however, let's get to the real deal, the heart and soul of this book—before you build that website, let's talk about getting your site noticed and getting it found so the search engines can send people to your site!

JUST THE FACTS
- Don't lose focus when designing a website: a website is for one purpose and one purpose only, and that's to get people to get in touch with you!

- Fancy is never better: plain is best here! Avoid whiz-bang Flash sites, and get a good designer to make a clean, simple, functional web site to convert leads. Be sure it is device responsive.

-Blogs are a vital part of a website's success: make yours the home page, or at least featured prominently on the home page!

- Following up is absolutely critical: you should have automated systems in place that follow-up with your patients the moment they get in touch with you.

Chapter 3: **Words, Words, Words: How to Choose the Right Keywords to Promote Your Business**

Having a website is all well and good, but it doesn't do much for you if nobody visits it. We'll have to get Google to notice you and rank you highly, and we'll do this using targeted keywords. We aren't going to make this a complicated discussion, but it is an important concept to understand.

What are keywords, you ask? Keywords are the words (either one word or multiple words) that users type into Google before they click search. A multiple-word keyword, like "Laser Cataract Surgery" or "Eye Care Clinic", is called a long-tail keyword phrase. When a user enters one of these keyword phrases, they will get back what Google thinks is most relevant to their search; more specifically, Google returns what it thinks are the best search results for the specific keyword phrase that the user entered in the search box.

Keywords must be included in the text of each of your web pages, otherwise they are buzz words; therefore meaningless!

That, in a nutshell, is what a keyword is. Our questions, however, are a tad more complicated: What keywords should we use? What keywords will get Google to notice that you are the best search result for a specific keyword phrase?

We have many clients who choose to have us do all of their Internet marketing for them. When we sit down at the table to discuss our plans for their Internet marketing strategies, there are two mistakes we see almost every time when we start talking about keywords:

1) Our new Client will be very excited to show us that they're ranking #1 for their particular domain name, like "www.RobertsonClinic.com"; the absolute worst domain name. Nobody cares about Robertson anything except you. The search engines will disregard Robertson. Clinic is confusing to the search engines; what type of clinic? To that point start listing all of the

types of clinics you can think of. The client is so excited, in fact, that it's almost tough to tell them that that's nothing to be excited about: next to nobody is searching for their exact clinic name on the Internet. If they are, it means they already know the clinic and know what the clinic does. Not to mention that Google and the other search engines do a pretty good job of making sure that your website is going to rank high on your clinic name by people who search within 25 miles of your location.

Never forget: you're using the Internet to get new patients who are trying to solve a problem that you and your clinic can solve; in short, you need to present an attractive solution to people with problems. People need help with "cataracts", "dry eye problems", "what is pink eye" or "how do I get pink eye"; these are the keywords people are putting into the search box! Nobody's looking for "Jones, Smith, and Johnson LLC", they're looking for "cataracts" or "dry eye", things that a clinic can provide a solution for. You want to rank for these keywords, and not for your business name!

2) The other big mistake we see made all the time is clinics ranking in terms that only make sense to someone who works in that particular industry. One of the ones we've seen very frequently lately is the keyword phrase; "RLE surgery"; Refractive Lens Exchange. Not many people know that Refractive Lens Exchange surgery is an option, and though they might learn about this term and start searching for that term in the future they're not doing so in great numbers right now. What the ideal prospect is typing in is "How can I correct my blurry vision?"; "How can I afford the type of corrective measures necessary?". People may not understand the terminology " Refractive Lens Exchange " but they do have a general idea that it might be what they're trying to look for; what they're really looking for is someone to help with correcting their vision.

The most important thing to remember in keyword selection is this: you must look at keywords from the user's perspective. You can't expect them to search for the terms you believe they're going to be able to define. For example, don't ever go to your industry association definitions for keywords—unless, of course, it's to see which keywords not to use! It's a trap that many people fall into all the time, and you've got to watch out for it.

Even we're not immune to it—we deal heavily in search and social media Internet marketing, and when we're not careful sometimes we find ourselves using terms people wouldn't use and don't care about: SEO, social media measurement. These are things our clients would never type in! They would type in something like "I want to get more patients" instead, and so those are the keywords we really care about.

These are the two big pitfalls that we see with most clinics that we work with, and they both stem from one thing: A lack of knowledge.

Specifically, the knowledge of what people are searching for. There are a number of tools that exist out there, but they are changing all the time.

These various online tools are helpful, and Ophthalmologists who know how to use them will really benefit from the services they provide; the best (and fastest) way, however, to find the right keywords is just to ask your family and friends. Think back to the first chapter, when we said that it's ordinary people that are using Google; that's as true for keyword usage as it is for research methods. Ask your friends, colleagues, and neighbors for help. Ask people who know you to explain to a friend what you do and ask to listen in. They will use plain English terms to describe your practice, and those are the terms that ordinary people are going to pop into that search box.

The reason this works is because it gets into the mind of a patient. If you gave a 60-second description of what you do to a patient, and then they turn around and tell that to a friend, it's not going to sound the same—in fact, odds are it'll be very different indeed!

What you're looking for in keyword selection is not how you describe your business, it's how patients and prospects describe it. If you're not ranking on the keywords that people are searching for, nobody's going to find you.

This might be a little overwhelming, but don't worry, we're not saying that you have to nail this on the first try and you can't change keywords over time. It's not the end of the world if you choose the wrong keyword on Day 1; keywords can be modified, refined, or even completely switched out altogether. Don't over think your keyword selection to the point that you freeze; start off by asking your neighbors and friends, as we described above. This is a very good method to finding keywords initially, and as you get more advanced you can start using some of the tools we talked about above to refine your keyword selection. Those tools will definitely benefit, but they're not crucial right out of the gate.

Start simply, as described above, and slowly grow in complexity as you master each step of the process.

Another way we use internally to refine keyword selection even further, is to use Google's "Related Searches" tool. This will give you an idea of what others are searching for when they search for your keywords, potentially giving you an insight into related terms that you may not have thought of.

Another important tool in your keyword research arsenal is the Google Keyword Tool (GKT for short). the GKT is important because although the Related Searches tool gives you suggestions, the GKT gives you returns for how many people per month are actually searching for that keyword. This is across the entire US, so you're going to have to make an educated (and usually valid) assumption that those will work in your locality very similarly to the way they work nationally. To stick to our earlier example, let's type in two terms: "cataract surgery" and "RLE surgery".

You'll notice that "cataract surgery" gets almost eight times as many searches as "RLE surgery". In fact, "RLE surgery" is small enough that you may not even want to initially target it. You can assume that in your locality these numbers will probably translate fairly well. It's not a given, and there's not a great tool right now for pinpointing exact numbers of local searches, but you need to assume that the national numbers will, more or less, apply reasonably well to your local searches.

If you really want a good idea of how many local searches those national numbers signify, you can do a rough calculation: take the last census date for the total US population and take the census of your location. Divide your location by the total population and it'll give you a rough estimate of the percentage of total population-multiply that times the keywords to get your number.

For example: Let's say you live in a city with one million people. The US has 300 million, by last count, which means your city has 1/300th of the amount of searches. "eye care" returns 300k hits per month, so we can assume that your locale's getting about 1000 searches per month on that keyword. It's not exact, but it's a very good guesstimate and is often more spot-on than you'd expect!

NOTE:
Do not think that bigger is always better! Sometimes, it's better to go after an easily-dominated keyword.

The other pitfall that clinics make is they typically want a neat, catchy name or their clinic name in the URL. If you want to rank really well, you're going to have to make your URL keyword rich.

Here's an example: Let's say you're an Ophthalmologist in Dallas, Texas, and you've decided on the keyword phrase "Best Cataract Surgeon Dallas". A great URL for your website, then, would be "http://www.BestCataractSurgeonDallas.com". (Authors Note: Use what we call Camel Case Lettering; upper and lower case, it is easier for your prospect to see and understand.) That's going to help tremendously in your efforts to rank high on Google. We realize that that's not a pretty name, and if you want to have your clinic name website URL for business cards and marketing materials you still can: It's both cheap and trivial to have multiple domain names, and you can easily have your webmaster redirect "http://www.johnsonandsmithllc.com" to "http://www.Best CataractSurgeonDallas.com" and still reap the benefits of the keyword-rich URL while having a professional URL on your business cards.

A keyword-rich URL is one of the first things you can do to influence your Google search rankings. We'll talk about other methods to rocket you to the top, of course, but if you start this process without a keyword-rich URL, it's going to be a very steep uphill battle. Do yourself a favor and start with a keyword-rich URL- it's very helpful and makes everything down the line much, much easier!

Niching
With this knowledge comes another facet of Internet marketing you need to know about: niching. As you may have guessed from that specific URL, you can't be highly ranked in everything. Unless you're a general practice Physician in a small town, there's going to be a ton of other doctors vying for that top spot in many different keywords and you're going to want to select some specialty or niche to focus on.

This isn't to say that you can't do other things or cross-sell once you get your patient, but you definitely have to step back and do some business strategy when it comes to niching.

Where is most of your revenue coming from? Where do you want it to come from? What's the most profitable aspect of your clinic? Some things require a significant amount of time, while there are other things that can just be reviewed while the staff does most of the actual work: the second is often more profitable.

What it comes down to is this: To dominate online, you have to know where you want to go and focus on one thing. Find something that you'd be happy with if 95% of your business came from that one thing. It's there that you're going to want to start in regards to your keywords.

Dominating the search rankings under eye care, cataract surgery, Medicare benefits, etc. and so forth all at once is going to be really hard, if not outright impossible. Start with the most important one, the one where you want to go: it might not be where you started, but it has to be where you want to go—the niche that you want to dominate in the future. Dominating that one keyword phrase means owning that particular source of business in your town.

In keeping with our earlier eye care example: let's say you want to dominate the keyword "cataract surgery". You'd make a keyword-rich URL out of that keyword-rich phrase, and then proceed to dominate the search rankings with your carefully crafted process, honed razor-sharp to focus on that particular niche.

Once you've narrowed down between 3-5 keyword phrases with a few words in them each, you'll want to make sure those keyword phrases are in your title tag in your website and that title tag starts ALWAYS with those keywords. You want the title tag to start with the keywords, move into the location, and end with the business name. Don't lead with your business name- the business name will come along for the ride.

It's all over your website, and people (and Google) aren't going to miss it. Start instead with the important keywords, and make sure those are peppered all throughout your site.

WARNING
Don't overdo it! Google is looking for real people with real content, and not automatons who simply spew out keywords nonstop. There's a joke in the Search Engine Optimization world about this:

Q: How many Search Engine experts does it take to change a light bulb?

A: Light. Bulb. Lamp. Fluorescent. Incandescent. LED, Flashlight...

The joke is light-hearted, but the message is clear: don't over-saturate! Be sure to use keywords and not buzzwords. Make sure your keywords hover around 4% density in the page text, which is the optimal percentage for keywords to words. (OK, we said we wouldn't try to confuse you about terms like keyword density and we just brought it up... we apologize, though you now know the specific data if you choose to use it. However, stick with talking about your subject in a natural way and this will just work itself out.)

Another very, very important thing to think about in this strategy is whether or not you're in an area where someone else is already dominating that larger keyword phrase. If someone's dominating the keyword phrase you want, you have to focus on smaller subsets of that keyword phrase: if you can dominate 2 or 3 smaller keyword phrases, you may end up actually getting more patients than the clinic that just went after that larger, broader term.

Those are, in effect, the two separate strategies you have to look at from an inside perspective. Everything in this book is important to understand for Ophthalmologists, because it makes you more knowledgeable. It enables you to do it yourself, or be savvy when you hire a business to do it for you. If you hire an outside business, you'll be able to make sure it's not just a webmaster who puts up a quick website but somebody who will ask these tough questions and really help you to think through the right online strategy for you. Just like the duplicate content we mentioned in Chapter One, there are lots of people just trying to sell something quick and dirty instead of doing things the right way—don't get fooled, and don't go into any negotiations without knowing what your marketing business should provide you.

Once you've got your keywords, your domain name, and your website ready, it's time to step up your game. Now, we're going to get into blogging to get ranked as well as more advanced local search techniques!

JUST THE FACTS
- Keywords are important; don't bother with trying to rank for your business name. Rank with keywords that get traffic and are terms that ordinary users are searching for!

- Incorporate your keywords into your website, and have a webmaster forward a professional-looking URL to the keyword rich one!

- Specialize, specialize and specialize: don't go for the broad market. Find your niche or specialty and aim towards that!

- Leverage your marketing tools, especially the people around you: they are, for the most part, representative of your patients and can offer insight into how your patients would search for you.

- Be natural! Google and Bing don't like keyword stuffing; don't ever go over 4% keyword density. Just write naturally, and almost always you'll have a good amount of keyword density with a natural reading flow.

Chapter 4: **Let's Get Local: Blogging and Advanced Local Search Techniques**

If you've been following this guide thus far, you've got a pretty reasonable setup going. In fact, you're probably better off than anybody who just threw up a website to have an Internet presence, and you're definitely better off than anyone who has refused the transition to web-based marketing. You may even have pulled a lead or two just from having the website, and you're considering putting your Google Places / Google + Local page up right away and watch your site skyrocket to the top of those local search returns!

We like your style, but hold on to your seat—your site's still small-fry! In this chapter, we're going to figure out how to make your local clinic big-time on the web using some more advanced local search techniques!

Blogging

Google has said emphatically that they're going to give stronger credit to resources that are both relevant to the user and current. This makes sense, given the overall makeup of the Internet: new content ages quickly, and very often newer info is far more useful to a person searching than old info. This problem is usually dealt with by adding new content to static web pages, but this method is time-consuming and more trouble than it's worth.

Our solution? Blogging.

It is true that blogging has become the online activity-du-jour on the Internet—it seems that everyone and their cat has one, and sometimes several. The fact of the matter is, however, that blogging has become a powerful force on the Internet; it also has one distinct advantage for us in that it's by far the easiest, most convenient, and most effective way to add new, updated content to your website. You don't have to go in and change copy all the time, you don't have to deal with static pages, HTML (hyper-text markup language), and minor edits, you just have to update your blog every now and then.

It's especially helpful when you consider Google's other preference in high-ranking Google search results: steady, relevant content. There's no "magic bullet" or fast-track way to get to the top of the Google search rankings; in this case, slow and steady wins the race. Blogging is absolutely, positively 100% all about this; it's essentially a vehicle to allow you to easily make regular, useful updates to keep your site both relevant and full of a steady stream of content.

To that end, there is a minimum amount of blog posts you should be putting out each week. Because of Google's preference for updated, steady content, you should be blogging at the very least once per week, and each blog post should be between about 250-800 words; they can be longer but they don't need to be, and they definitely shouldn't be any shorter than 250 words or Google may mark them down as non-useful. Note: 250 words is only about three minutes of talking.

This may seem daunting to many, and understandably so; the thought of composing another written piece every week isn't appealing to many folks out there. If you truly think about it, however, once a week isn't too bad; that's only four times a month, and if you make a schedule and stick to it you'll find that blogging really isn't the chore you thought it would be.

If you're finding that you have time for more, it's beneficial to up your blog posts to twice a week; that's the optimal number in this sort of situation, and it'll most likely net you the most positive credit when Google compiles its local search returns. Twice a week, however, is plenty; don't go over that! Some people come into this with a very linear mindset. They think that since 2 is better than 1, 5 must be better than 2. It's not, and you'll experience a very diminished rate of return in this regard; 2 blog posts a week is much better than 1, but 5 blog posts a week is barely better than 2. Bottom line is this: If you're spending more than 2 times a week blogging, there are other, better things you could be doing with that time!

Blog Subjects

Having a blog is all well and good, but a blog without useful, relevant content is hardly a blog at all! To that end, you're going to need to fill your blog with useful, quality content that maximizes the amount of utility Google perceives in your site. Here are the three main content points you should be hitting in your blog posts:

1) Talk About What You Do

This one may seem pretty obvious, but it's worth mentioning: talk about what you do, not who you are. Don't talk about yourself, how long your clinic has been around, how great your service is; this isn't going to help you any. You need to fill your blog posts with quality content that relate to the services you do, quality content is valuable or useful to the user. Let's say you're an Ophthalmologist involved in Medicare benefits and a new law or change happened in Medicare benefits regulation. A perfect blog post would be a post covering these changes or relevant info pertaining to them; you could title it "Medicare benefits answers you need to know" and phrase it as an easygoing, inside look at how the Medicare benefits have changed and what that could mean for anyone looking to act on them.

2) Plugged in: Talk About Local Events

#1 on this list may seem obvious to most, but this trick isn't: of all of them, this is the super-ninja secret of Internet marketing! The trick is this: talk about local events! Blogging about things going on and tying them back into what you do is a great, great way to make Google take notice and gain credit with them in the local search return results. A good example of this would be if you lived in a city and there's a big event; talk about the big event and how it related to your community. Let's say you live in a college town and every Saturday during football season the town quadruples in size. It's an event that polarizes many a college town- local residents are, in general, proud / frustrated about the big event, think it's good / bad for business? Think the traffic isn't worth the amount of money the game brings into the town? Do you have suggestions for parking or must hit restaurants or activities for the in-bound football fans?. You can write a blog post about this, and it'll help you with Google because Google will see that you're a part of the community and (more importantly) the blog posts gives Google lots of keyword clues about your location, really helping you to rise to the top in your location!

Additionally, don't feel pressured to make the blog post about medical issues in the community. In fact, shy away from it- these local community posts are as valuable in their own way as the medical posts you make, and someone who searches you will have plenty of time browsing your site and blog to see your other posts and find out about what you do and how you do it. This helps your clinic come out on top in the location it's in, because of the connection and keyword clues mentioned above; if somebody searches for "cataract surgery Dallas TX" you'll show up because both your blog posts and your location-based (Dallas, TX), community-based blog posts as well. Many, many people don't do this, and that's understandable; on the surface, it doesn't make sense to talk about things that aren't related to what you do.

TIP:
You can always refer to yourself with your keywords! Don't overdo it, but it's perfectly fine to use things like "As an Ophthalmologist in Dallas, Texas, I'm always surprised when...". That's the best of both worlds!

Another great tip is to be proactive- go to a local newspaper site, see what they're covering, and link back to the newspaper site and talk about it. It's easy research!

This also has the added advantage of making you seem more likeable and down-to-earth, which is always a huge bonus in patient interaction.

When someone finds your blog and reads through it, it'll be enjoyable- he or she will be getting not just practical medical advice but also feel some connection to you as well. When they read your blog, they won't see just another faceless _____ - they'll read your blog posts about the community and think "Gee, this person has personality. They seem to really know what they are talking about,

AND they are also a part of my community and seem really invested in it."

That person is more likely to pick up the phone and give you a call, and you just got a warm lead by being a personable blogger who talks about the community!

3) Be Natural
This ties into the last point—be natural! You don't always have to sound like the smartest person in the world. This isn't to say you should be sloppy or stupid, but you shouldn't sound like a king preaching from atop the ivory tower either. Your patients (and Google) like to see content and blog posts that appear and are from normal people. Conversation, stories, and anecdotes are all things they like to index; conversing on your blog makes you more reachable and more indexable.

This isn't just a Google-specific tactic, either; your patients will love you for it as well, as we mentioned above. It's always been a general marketing strategy to be likeable; it's the age-old marketing concept that people are more likely to work with those they know, like and trust.

They see your blog posts and say "Hey! This person knows what they're talking about and likes what I like." They see a real person, with a real family, and it makes them feel more comfortable working with you. A blog is the best place to do this, so plan out your blog structure accordingly. You don't have to do 52 weeks of straight specialty eye care; you can do every now and then an informal, "hey, somebody asked me about this the other day and I thought I'd talk about it" post.

A good rule of thumb, if you're doing the minimum 4 times a month, is to split it up half and half: twice a month goes to business posts, and twice a month goes to local, personal stories. People like to know people, it's a fact of interaction; it will greatly help your sales when they feel that they know you more personally. This tactic may feel a little too touchy-feely for some, but don't knock it: it works very well, and blogging is a great way to do it! It drives patients and will improve your ranking, which is of course a major goal of this book.

What you should really take home from this chapter is not to underestimate the power of the local connection. We've had clients that have followed this process to the letter, and their specialty posts only gained a few hits and comments. It was their local stories and blog posts, however, which became a focal point. Conversations about how bad traffic was when a big event happened got tons of links, comments, and opinions from across the board.

In the end, this is what you want: it's the reason for this section and the reason you're branching out into the community. Not only does this sort of activity tied into your locality keywords mean big index boosts from Google, it also means very effective general marketing: it makes you a real person that people feel comfortable calling, one of the best advantages you can have in our modern, very skeptical era!

JUST THE FACTS

- Blogging is key to the success of your marketing campaign: make sure to blog at least once a week with a post that is between 250 and 800 words. If possible, blog twice a week; this is the optimal number, and blogging more than twice a week won't help you more.

- You don't have to make every blog about eye care; you should alternate them between eye care and events in the community.
- Be natural; this will help you be more accessible to your patients, and thus garner more page views and attention from people looking to comment on the blog as well as make you more viewable and indexable by search engines.

Chapter 5: **Let's Get Social: Using Facebook, LinkedIn, and the Rest**

We know some of you are snickering. We know some of you are sitting in your home or offices, having read the title of this particular chapter, and are thinking "Twitter! That can't possibly help me."

Don't laugh just yet, however: We know how silly Twitter sounds. We know the derision it's received from all sides, including our friends and the media; the fact of the matter is, however, that Twitter is relevant. As much as it pains us to say, Twitter may be one of the more important factors that figures into your Internet marketing strategy.

So you better get tweeting!

Why Social Media?

Simply put: Social media is starting to become a very powerful force in how Google is determining what is relevant online. The Internet is full of bots, scammers, and article spinners, and many links out there are links to irrelevant or otherwise spammy articles. Social media, however, does the vetting by itself: Users of social media sites aren't going to share spammy links with each other, they're going to share real content. As a result, Google has realized that indexing and calculating relevancy from social media is very beneficial, since social media (in general) has real people posting real content, content that was valuable enough to warrant a "hey, check this out" from one person to another.

Some of us have been trying to avoid social media for one reason or the other; privacy, general lack of interest, or whatever other reason you may have avoided it thus far. The statistics on social media and Internet marketing, however, can't be denied: for example, By 2010 Gen Y will outnumber Baby Boomers....96% of them have joined a social network. These are the people that look and by ignoring the social media segment you're basically ignoring their primary mode of access.

- The average time on Google is three minutes. The average time on Facebook is thirteen minutes.

- Facebook, as of this writing, has over 1.11 billion users. To put that into perspective, that means Facebook has more users than the US population; this is very important in terms of saturation.

What these statistics should show you is that social media is a very, very powerful force in today's cultural mindset, and it's only getting stronger. Social media is here to stay, and more and more people every day are joining it and receiving advice from their friends and family about great stories or services that they received.

Google has been taking notice of that and responding accordingly, and so should you. In this chapter, we're going to take a look at social networks and your strategy for them: we're going to figure how just to approach these social media websites and use them to help Google notice you!

The Social Networks

In the social media game, there are currently three huge players that we're going to focus on: Facebook, Twitter, and LinkedIn. This isn't to say you should ignore the other social media networks out there; they're still important, and in fact location-based social media like Foursquare and Facebook Places are very useful too. You may want to have a presence in those, and other minor social networks as well, like YouTube, Google+, etc.

For the core of our marketing strategy, however, we're going to focus on the big three. This focus will give you the most coverage and best ROI in terms of time spent on marketing, and so it's how we'll proceed!

Facebook

Facebook's the biggest social media in the room, the 800-pound gorilla; everybody knows and uses it, so you're going to need to capitalize on that. The first thing you should have is a fan page, and so we'll take a look at how to create one and how to link it into your overall Internet marketing strategy.

TIP:
Many of you will be scared of Facebook's privacy implications. It's very important to note that your business fan page is NOT your personal page. It's not connected to your personal page, it's not the same thing as your personal page, and nothing you post on your personal page will appear on your business page or vice versa. They are completely separate entities! For those you of you resisting joining Facebook / are afraid your fan page will expose your personal page, fear not: none of your personal information will go on your fan page, and your privacy is safe.

Your Facebook Fan Page

A fan page, quite simply, represents your business. Facebook fan pages can have dynamic pages that offer info about your business- you're going to want someone to build a custom iframe on the landing page for your fan page; your web developer or webmaster should be able to do this pretty easily. When new visitors come to the fan page they will see the information in the iframe, which will be an opt-in box and benefit information; this will be very similar to the calls to action you have on your main website- "3 things to know before you call an Ophthalmologist", that sort of thing.

The great part of this fan page is that you're adding new patients onto an email marketing list through a social media channel. It's a very organic way of getting warm leads and targeted marketing. These people are already in the social media world, surfing around, and in their social network traversal they stumble on your fan page and think "Wow! I might need an Ophthalmologist for my cataracts".

In fact, the #1 growing demographic of Facebook is 25-34 and 35-54 year old females. This is a massive, growing target market for many, many people who need a doctor for all kinds of reasons. It's definitely the right mix of people with the money and the motive to hire a doctor, and your fan page on Facebook will be a great place for them to get in touch with you regarding their problems.

While you're creating your Facebook fan page, don't forget about your Facebook Places page as well. The location-based aspect of this is really attractive, especially because of the proliferation of mobile phones. More and more people are buying smartphones and more and more things are going mobile; with a Places page, people can check in and see what's around them, and you can offer specials through this mode of delivery. At least get on this radar, but you can take it further- be creative! Combine things like your Fan page and Places page, and figure out ways to synergize the two to make an effective marketing vehicle!

This is perhaps the most important thing to know about social media in general; all of these things can be linked together in different ways.

There are so many options for managing Fan pages and Places pages that it's vital you have a professional who knows how to set up social media correctly. Barring that, you need to get online and do some extensive research into establishing the proper social media channels; it's not something you can just cobble together quickly.

Once you've got your Fan page and Places set up, it's time to move on!

Twitter

Twitter—one of the oldest social networks out there, and perhaps one that inspires the most reluctance to join. It's been much vilified by the media and our peers, but the fact remains that Twitter is important: it's the most open social network out there.

In fact, this is the whole reason Twitter is so important. Every single tweet (a "tweet" is an individual Twitter post) is indexed by Google. Other social networks, like Facebook and LinkedIn, need a username and password to see most of their content; with Twitter, there's no requirement to log in to see individual tweets. What this means is that Google can index all the tweets out there, and this means that Twitter informs Google page rankings enormously; Google is using people's tweets to help gauge the importance of pages all around the

Internet. Pages with lots of links from Twitter, for example, are going to increase its importance: you don't want to be spammy, but you do want to take advantage of this fact.

That's the basis of most of your Twitter interaction, when it's all said and done: taking advantage of Twitter's ability to generate constant content without coming across as being spammy. You can't just blast out links to your blog articles all day; a stream of useless / irrelevant content from you (or rehashed content) isn't going to help you to increase your page rank.

Much like the techniques described in "Go Local Big-time", you're going to want to create a bunch of tweets about local things like events as well as topical content like minor changes, changes that would be important or useful for people to know. Your tweets are going to be composed of similar content to your blogs, except shortened down to the 140 character limit per tweet, and sent out once or twice a day.

This may seem as daunting as the blogging, especially considering the daily frequency of the tweets. Truth be told, however, 140 characters is not that much at all, and you don't have to sit by the computer and send them out one by one; there are tons of websites / programs that let you schedule tweets, including HootSuite (http://hootsuite.com), SocialOomph (http://www.socialoomph.com), and more. You can sit down for an hour and write enough tweets for a week or two, schedule them, and forget about them until the next week when you sit down to write some more!

Don't be tempted just to tweet an exact duplicate of your blog posts or articles! Your tweets should be on the same content as your blog posts, but they shouldn't be copied and pasted straight from the blog. What you can do, however, is to link back to your blog from your tweets: in fact, this is not only permissible but encouraged! There are many, many plug-in for countless blogging platforms that enable you to automatically send out a tweet with a link to your blog post every time you post a new blog post. Take advantage of that to generate links to your blog posts—that's not spammy since it's only once or twice a week, and it's a great tool for slowly and steadily creating links back to your blog. There are also plug-ins for Facebook as well—make sure when you post a blog, it's getting automatically posted to your Twitter and Facebook page!

LinkedIn

In the social media circles, LinkedIn is often completely overshadowed by its bigger social media cousins Facebook and Twitter. It is instead regarded as just a professional or resume-sharing site and nothing more; this is a big misstep for many, as LinkedIn is an enormous cash cow if used properly. For starters, LinkedIn itself is no slouch in terms of financial recognition; now publicly traded (LNKD), Linked In has a market cap of $8-$10 billion (or $70-$100 per user)—making it a very formidable, fast-growing contender in the social media sphere. Additionally, LinkedIn has an added attraction to us that isn't related to its market share. Because of LinkedIn's status as a site for professionals and resume-swapping, the average LinkedIn user is far more likely to be a potential patient because of the means / motive aspect we described earlier with Facebook.

1.   Over one fifth of users are Middle Management level or above
2.   Almost 60% have a College or Post Grad degree
3.   Average Household Income is $88,573.
4.   All of these numbers are higher than published statistics for Wall Street Journal, Forbes, or Business Week.

Put simply, LinkedIn users are wealthier and have more need for services and non-useful demographics, like teenagers, aren't crowding the LinkedIn user space to post pictures of their friends and pets. LinkedIn is composed of your potential patients interacting with each other, looking for professionals and just waiting to be introduced to your business.

Press Releases

This isn't really social media, but we're going to incorporate it into this section because it deals with controlling a message that goes out and can get shared and receive comments; in a sense, the medium of the Internet itself is social. PR is also one of the few places where Google expects duplicate content; the more duplicated/shared the press release is, the more important the content must be.

15 Great Press Release Ideas:

1.   Someone in your company is speaking at an industry conference, local chamber, rotary club, etc.
2.   You hire someone new into your company
3.   Someone is promoted
4.   You join an association (local or national)
5.   You start offering a new service or product
6.   New office space or additional office added
7.   Successful patient -- create a Case Study and send out press release
8.   Awards received or recognition from local or national industry or association
9.   Employee or officers named to charity benefit or non-profit board
10.   Large sponsor of a charity benefit
11.   New Business contract awarded
12.   Having a big promotion or sweepstakes or contest - issue a press release
13.   Your product and services tie into a big current event news item (new government law, health discovery, tax time, new hot-topic movie release, etc.)
14.   Launch of a new website (hint, hint)
15.   The release of your special report (hint)

There are both paid and free press sites out there; the paid press sites are worth the money sometimes because they go out to Associated Press and other big name news wires, like Yahoo and Google News. The more that your story gets out there, the more possibility it is that it could get picked up; a local paper could see that press release and pick up the story, for example, and that's a great thing to take advantage of. The problem of duplicate content goes out the window because duplicate content is expected in press releases, and often the big names, like Associated Press and Reuters, even source duplicate content!

GOOGLE+:

What makes Google+ different from Facebook, Linkedin, Youtube and Twitter?

This is not Google's 1st attempt at social. There are many social networks, but let's focus on the big 4 Facebook, LinkedIn, YouTube and Twitter. Understanding how these sites operate helps explain Google+.

YouTube – I make a video. You search for it and can watch, share, or comment on my video. As a search based network this is the most open network of them all. Few people use the subscribe function as a social element.

Linkedin – Use to be: Here is my resume please hire me - Now is: I need a job, I collaborate with my colleagues & vendors to learn and grow in groups, and I get answer / questions. The most closed network of the 4, you must know my email, already have worked with me, or be in a group with me to connect.

Twitter – I can push information out to many people and this information can be spread quickly. Google indexes this network, which is a bonus. As many people as are on Twitter can follow my updates. You can follow me and I do not need to follow you. Information is sent out in short burst and interaction takes place both on Twitter (in a short conversation style) and off Twitter (follow this link to see this video, read my blog, etc)

Facebook - The current king of social media. Facebook is about "friendships". You and I must mutually like each other to share information. I can post information with hopes that this information is seen on your News Feed. There is no guarantee my information will be seen by my friends. Facebook controls information and uses an algorithm called Edge to determine what information they believe I want to see. There is a great business component with Pages (formally fan pages).

Google+ What makes you so different?

From a big picture Google+ is all about connecting all of your computer uses both online and offline in one place. We are talking cloud on a major scale. We are talking about your documents, spreadsheets, applications, videos, everything being available in one location and everything being one click from something you can share.

This brings us to the MAJOR DIFFERENCE of Google+

So this is great, I can share all my information from my blog to my expense report, but I don't want to share everything with the world. My mom does not need to know about everything about work and my patients don't want to know about my personal life.
Google+ plus has created a revolutionary function called CIRCLES. Circles control both the stream of information out and in. People you connect with are organized into different circles.

How do Circles work and why are they important?

1) You can create any circle you want. Examples of my circles include: Following, Friends, Best Friends, Employees, Clients, Vendors, Very Smart Marketing People, Fellow Marketers, Funny Peeps and Family.

2) The people you connect with can be in multiple circles. Some people that are Very Smart Marketing People are also my Friends.

3) I can choose to send information to one, or more, circles. This information will appear on their wall or can be sent as a message. The great thing is if I share something with my client circle only they see it and no one else sees that post on their feed.

Maybe we just got back from a family vacation and I want to share the photos with my family and friends but do not want to bother my vendors, clients, and the general public with the images.

4) I can choose to see information from one or more circles in my feed. Instead of being told what content an algorithm thinks I would like to see, I can choose my content feed based on my circles. This allows me to quickly and easily navigate from one set of feeds to the next.

Since you can have people in multiple circles, I know that I am seeing what I want from whom I want.

Here are a few other features to Google+

• Google Hangout. Google+ will allow you to connect with up to 100 people on live video chat at the same time. The feature is smooth and audio is good. A real great way to connect with people for virtual meetings. The best part of this feature is the person talking gets the main screen.

• Larger image and video display on the wall. When you post a video or images they are about 3 times larger on the wall when compared to Facebook.

• Easy navigation to all of Google's functions. While on Google+ you can search the web, see your gmail messages, and access your Google Documents.

• Simple share option. This is very similar to Facebook, Google uses both a +1 button (similar to Facebook's like) and a "share this post" option.

• 1 click and you can add someone. If you see a name in a post, find someone in your friends feed, or stumble upon someone of interest you can add them without navigating to their page. This is very convenient. When you hover over their name a box appears giving you the option to add them to a circle.

Setting up Google+ is simple. Similar to other social media outlets, there is an area for information about you, pictures, website URLs, and basic data. As always, only share what you are comfortable sharing. Make sure your about me section has benefits to working with you and keywords for your industry. Like LinkedIn there is a title there that you should also include keywords about your area of practice. The difficult part about social media is that it is rapidly changing. We have created an area where you can go to get the most up-to-date information about social media and the changes to the various networks.

With that, our foray into social media has ended; next up on our list is directory listings!

Just the Facts:
- Social media is one of the most important forces in marketing today: it can't afford to be ignored, and you need to set up strategies for dealing with it.

- The three biggest social media players right now are Facebook, Twitter, and LinkedIn: you need to have pages for them and have a system set up on your blog that pushes blog updates to the respective social networks.

- Google+, though new, is rapidly growing: make sure to incorporate it into your marketing strategy!

- Press releases are an extremely important part of your online marketing strategy, so much so that you should have your marketing business do it for you and cut down on the immense amount of time you're spending on it.

- Social media is rapidly changing, and no single strategy will stay effective forever; make sure to keep yourself updated to stay ahead of the game!

Chapter 6: **Out With the Old: How to Use Online Directories to Get More Patients**

If you've been an Internet user since the pre-search days, you'll recognize directory listings. Directory listings are, in short, the online version of the Yellow Pages: Super Pages, YellowPages.com, Yahoo Local, Bing Places, Google Places / Google + Local, etc.. These directories are commonly called "citations" by those in the Internet marketing and search marketing industry. There are hundreds of them across the Internet; there are, however, 15-20 major ones where you want to be listed. In addition to the main directories like MerchantCircle.com, SuperPages.com, Yelp.com, and Yahoo Local. The majority of these services allow for a free listing. You don't need to pay for these listings. The directories will tell you all kinds of reasons why you should pay; but don't!

You should not need anything more than that. Resist the urge and the follow-on emails and phone calls trying to up-sell you into a paid option. A paid listing or preferred listing may be right for you depending on your market, but do everything else first and after you have a baseline for your online success, test the gain in calls or emails you receive by opting for a paid enhancement to a directory listing. That way you can measure the real cost/benefit of the investment. Some directories, like InfoUSA, are even more influential and you must be sure your information is correct and optimized there because other directories pull information from them; in time, as other directories use the information there, your information will proliferate all over the Internet. Make sure it is the right information.

These directories/citations have risen to prominence lately because of Google's local search return policies, since Google has moved its local search returns to its main page, using Google Places / Google + Local. The algorithm that determines which Google Places / Google + Local business listings belong on the first page of Google search results takes a great deal of its weighting consideration by looking around the Internet to see if your business is listed elsewhere. If you're in 5, 10, or even 15 directory listings (with reviews in the local area) that's going to look very good in Google's ranking system. We'll get to reviews in the next chapter, but suffice it to say that directory listings with reviews are very helpful; if your competition is getting more reviews than you, you often won't make the first page and they will!

You're going to want to be on a great many directories; there are some services out there that will do this for you, but quite often the best way to do it is to do it manually. You really want to be in control of this—some services are pretty spotty in this regard, and they'll slip in shady techniques or insist that you stay out of the process. It's not that hard but time-consuming, and we recommend doing it manually; just go through the top 15-20 directory listings, enter in your data, put photos, and fill out the details as much as you can. Make sure to use keywords and geolocation in your description; geolocation is just an SEO term for city / state. In keeping with our Ophthalmology example, if you're a Ophthalmologist and your keywords are "cataract surgery", you could put in your description "cataract surgery in Dallas, Texas".

How to List Yourself

It's a pretty easy process to list yourselves, all things considered. You just have to go to these directories and their websites, and list yourself.

Some are paid, but many are free and just try to upcharge you with different services once you've listed yourself on the directories. You may be conflicted about these upcharges and paid directory listings, but they're really not necessary. Our experience is that, done correctly, you never need to pay for directory listings or any of the extra services the free ones offer you; judicious and skillful use of keywords and geolocation will be more than enough to bump you up to the top. We've had many, many clients top-ranked in Google Places / Google + Local who never paid for directory listings, and it's most likely the case that you'll never have to pay for a directory listing or upcharge either.

That is not to say that these additional paid services won't provide more traffic and patients to your clinic, but don't start there. Be warned, however: you will get multiple phone calls from those directories looking to sell you upcharges and service add-ons. Changes to Google and other advertising venues online have left many of these directories rethinking their business models and scrambling by the wayside; paying for a directory listing is no longer as necessary as it used to be. You'll have many directories telling you to upcharge this and upcharge that and pay for advertising, but don't do it: stay steadfast, keep on trucking, and you'll see that it wasn't necessary at all to pay for any services that the directory listings tried to offer you!

WARNING:

Big warning here! This is a problem that we run into with many local businesses. What happens is that often in a office, you have 3-4 doctors that are really in one office partnership; sometimes, each of them will go in and create their own listings, so you end up with multiple listings for each doctor and one for the office as a whole. When Google queries the directory listings, it gets confused at the multiple entries for the one address; it thinks it's an attempt to game the system and may ignore them all.

You want to go in and be very, very careful that you only have one listing; search for your address, business name, other people in the office, anything you can think of to identify multiple listings. If you do have multiple listings and didn't know it, delete them all! Get down to zero and start from scratch; it's much better that way. If for whatever reason you can't delete them all, at least get down to one and edit that one as best you can.

It used to be a big trick to list duplicate listings to boost search rankings, and so now Google cracks down on it very hard. Remember: duplicate listings are bad! Too many dupes, and Google completely ignores them all. Be very wary of this, and search hard for duplicate listings!

Another important thing to remember when you're doing directory listings is to make sure to use keywords and geolocation only in the short / long descriptions that the directory listings give you. Do not use keywords in your business name! This is why you have a keyword-rich URL; if the URL was the business name you'd have to use that and not get the keyword benefit. Google does not like to see business names stuffed with keywords and geolocation; that will definitely hurt you in the long run.

This can be turned to your advantage, depending on how dedicated you are to this strategy; some of our sharper clients have actually changed their business name to include keywords and geolocation, like "Cataract Surgeon of Georgia Business". This may recall the Yellow Pages game of putting A's in business names to get to the top of the listings, like "AA Best Eye Care of Dallas, Texas".

If your company name officially contains your keywords and location, Google is OK with that; what they're watching out for is obvious keyword stuffing like "Jones Smith and Barney Eye Care Clinic - cataracts - dry eye - Medicare benefits - Dallas TX". That's bad, and those keywords should go in your description and not in your business name.

If the directory listing has suggested keywords, consider using them; it probably looks very similar to the Yellow Pages categories you are used to seeing. Some places give you a chance to type in yours, in which case do so. Don't go crazy, however, because Google only values about 3-4 keywords; anything after that they consider gaming the system and just ignore.

Here is a list of directories that your business needs to be listed on.
1.   Google Places / Google + Local
2.   Yahoo!
3.   YellowBot
4.   Yelp
5.   White Pages
6.   MapQuest
7.   SuperPages
8.   CitySearch

9.   YellowBook
10.   Local.com
11.   MerchantCircle

There are about 40 more directory listings that we list our clients on. Some of these directory listings are more relevant today then a year from now. Do some research and find at least 15 more directories to list your business on top of the core 11 above.

Google Places / Google + Local

Google Places / Google + Local, though technically a listing, deserves a special mention here. The Google Places / Google + Local listing should be the absolute last thing you should create; get the rest of the directory listings in first, wait a month or so until you have a few reviews, and then create your Google Places / Google + Local page. This wait time is very important- it's so important, in fact, that if we meet clients who already have a Google Places / Google + Local listing before this structure is in place we sometimes advise them to delete it and start over unless it's already in the top 7 listings. If it's not on the first page, delete it, do this process, and then add it a month later.

The reason behind this is that when you create a Google Places / Google + Local page, it goes forth and looks for all the info about you:

Directory listings, blogs, reviews, etc. and so forth. If you've done all the things we've talked about it should help rocket way up to the top of the list once you create it; if you want to be on the first page, waiting those four weeks to make a Google Places / Google + Local listing makes a huge, huge difference in your ranking!

Also, another powerful, yet rarely discussed advertising medium is Pay Per Click advertising…the best example of which is Google AdWords. AdWords is pound-for-pound the single quickest way to get your business listed on Page #1 of Google. You can do it in 10 minutes or less. It will cost you a few dollars a day (when you know what you are doing). Or it could cost you thousands (if you don't). The key is to have your ads show ONLY in your geographical area.

Our recommendation is to find someone who is skilled at AdWords because it is an art and pay them to do your ads. It will pay off for you in the end.

Just the Facts:

- There are hundreds of directory listings out there; be smart and only join the 15-20 that are the biggest and most relevant (yelp, AVVO, etc.)

- You can pay people to put you on directories, but the best and cheapest way is to do it yourself. Most directories are free. They'll try to get you with up-sells and add-ons, but don't bother. They don't help.

- Don't put keywords in your business name in the directories; Google doesn't like it unless those keywords are officially part of your business name.

- You'll be tempted to put up a Google Places / Google + Local along with the directories, but don't. Since Google pulls information about you when you create the Google Places / Google + Local page, it's best to wait a month or so and create after you've gotten a few reviews.

Chapter 7: **In With the New: How to Use Online Reviews to Drive Your Marketing**

This part of the system really confuses some people, especially since reviews are created by patients. How can reviews make or break a search engine ranking? Sure, they might be helpful for patients talking to patients, but they surely can't influence Google's monstrous ranking machine in your favor. Can they?

As it turns out, they can and they do influence the ranking system. Very much so, in fact; Google uses reviews in order to judge the validity of the place in question. Put simply, if the location's been reviewed, someone's been there, and the review comments also give an indication of the quality of the location and whether or not it deserves to be ranked higher or lower. Many of these reviews allow reviewers to give star ratings, which are even more influential: Google scrapes these numbers automatically to do a sort of website litmus test, a judgment of whether or not the establishment is overall positive or negative.

In fact, Google has recently adjusted the Google Places / Google + Local page user interface to prominently display the "Write a review" button to specifically encourage reviews within Google's own systems.

Review sites are, in general, the directory listings we talked about earlier; Google uses the info to determine whether or not you're the best solution to the problem that the user is trying to solve. This is important- the whole idea of the ranking system and your marketing strategy is to make Google see that you are, in fact, the best solution to the problem!

Another key point to this strategy is that many of your competitors are simply not getting reviews at all. This is especially true in the Internet marketing strategies; we've done extensive research and hardly any of them are getting any reviews at all.

As a result, you don't need to get a billion reviews on your directory listings and Google Places / Google + Local page; you just need to have a little consistency and make sure you're getting a couple reviews a month on just 2 or 3 different directories (one of which must be Google Places / Google + Local).

To start, you're going to need to size up how many reviews you need to rank. Do some review research on your keywords; type them into Google and see how many reviews the top ranked results have. If they have five reviews, you need ten- if they have two hundred, well... you've got a lot of work to do! Typically, however, physicians have somewhere in the ten to twenty range when it comes to number of reviews (and many markets don't have any we have found). For the most part, in order to beat them at the rankings game, you'll need to have about double the amount of reviews they have.

Keep in mind that these are total reviews: for example, if you need twenty reviews, you can spread it over four months. That's just five reviews per month, which is certainly doable, and we'll talk about how to get those reviews in a second.

Review Sites

First things first, however, on which sites should you be focusing on getting reviews? There are tons of them out there, and some of them don't matter and some of them do.

How do you figure out which ones are worth your time and which ones aren't?

Thankfully, there's a fairly efficient way to do it. First off, half the work is done: many of these review sites are also directory listings, and you've already listed yourself on the top directory listings. What you have to do, then, is to do a Google keyword search in your location and go through the pages at the bottom.

Don't go digging too far; if you scroll down to the bottom, you'll see numbers as far as the mouse can click. For your part, you're just interested in the top 5 directories that are already listed; make a list of your directory listings and cross-reference which ones appear first in the Google keyword search. For example, if you are a Ophthalmologist in Denver Colorado, then you should Google " Ophthalmologist – your business name". Then look at the results and find the first 3-5 listings that refer to an online directory site like Yelp, CitySearch, or SuperPages. The 3-5 that appears first are the ones you're going to want to focus on.

It's also OK if you don't find 5; you may only find 2 or 3 at the beginning, and that's fine. This is normal- sometimes it can take search engines quite some time to properly index all the information out there. To give you some perspective, there are about ten thousand new websites created every day; this is a gigantic amount for search engines to index, and so often there's a lag time as the search engines crawl the pages and index them. Your mission here is to find the ones that are ranked, and of those find the top ranked ones; these are the ones where you're going to focus your review techniques!

TIP:
If there are a great number of reviews for your keyword niche, consider focusing on one or two. Ordinarily, clinics don't generally have to deal with this, since the healthcare market isn't normally saturated with reviews. If you have a competitor that's saturated with reviews, however, Google their keywords and see which review sites are consistently being pulled up the most; focus all your review efforts on those. As an example, if your keyword is "cataracts" and the majority of reviews are being pulled from CitySearch, then CitySearch is the best place to start.

Getting Reviews

Now that we've narrowed down our target directories, let's get reviews on them. We'll start with your current patients: it'll be easier to get reviews from them, as they're right in the middle of working with you.

It's important to note here that we understand that healthcare providers are, depending on the state, sometimes not allowed to ask for testimonials.

You need to understand this because this is important: you are not asking for a testimonial. We are very clear on this point: you are simply asking for someone to go to a website and put in a review. It's on a public forum where they could leave the review with or without your assistance. You're going to want to have a card produced that you hand to your patients as they walk out the door; this card will tell them where to go and how to write a review. This is absolutely crucial!

WARNING:
You cannot, under any circumstances, go in to these websites and create the reviews for your patients. They also can't give you the reviews and you write the reviews; Google will know from the IP address that these reviews are all coming from the same location and they will ignore it at best and hurt your ranking or get rid of your listing altogether at the worst. This is true even if they are real reviews that patients mailed you; a common scammer trick is to have teams of people writing multiple reviews, and as such Google is searching that spam out and penalizing that harshly. Under no circumstances should your patients write reviews from your location; they have to go to their computer at their house, business, or coffee shop and write the review there. This is vital!

But we have a way to do just that!

This also extends to other computers in your office. There is a common setup we see fairly often; businesses will have a "review" computer set up in the office, where patients can go and enter in a review. This falls into the same trap as the scenario above, and we always warn patients against this when we see it: Google is tracking these reviews, and even though it's not you typing, unfortunately, it's coming from the same place. Google can't distinguish these from scammers who employ that same trick, and thus having this "review station" isn't going to help you at all. They absolutely, positively have to do it on their computer in their home or business; there's no way around this and it's very important for you to remember this!

WARNING:
Be very, very, very careful about who you hire to do your review process! There are many services out there that will solicit you and claim to be able to get you lots of reviews. Very often, these services are near-spam type businesses that just create all the reviews themselves and post them from one IP address; not only is this not going to help you, this sort of review fabrication is against the law. You have to be very careful about who you consult and how; if you talk to a company that says they'll get you twenty reviews in a week, you should be very cautious. We've even seen reviews from businesses we've worked with that have used such services; the result shows 20 reviews for different businesses that are all just the same sentence with the business name replaced.

Do not use a service! If you absolutely must, make sure you build your process with a proven agency / partner. We provide our clients with an entire review process.

As an example of this, we have a process where we do calling / mailers for the client depending on their individual needs. We keep close communication with the client and have an active role due to the nature, sensitivity, and importance of reviews; this is how your service, if you use one, should treat you. Make sure the service keeps very close to your business and ultimately gives your business the ultimate control over the review process. This is a crucial part of hiring a service—don't forget it whenever you're looking around for these agencies or services.

The best way to get reviews, as mentioned above, is to hand out your card. Don't stop there, however: another great way is mailing or emailing patients asking for reviews. Make it a team effort- insert into the email where you're ranking and where your competitors are ranking, and explain that you want to get to the top and get reviews as well.

Remember that this isn't all about Google Places / Google + Local; we want to send people to a few different directories. You do of course want reviews going to Google Places / Google + Local as well, but you need to diversify: have cards with other review sites on them as well, such as Yelp, CitySearch, and the others that you've identified in your target directory listings. Try not to put them all on one card, however: it looks cramped, awkward, and unprofessional. A card per review site looks much better, and it'll work better in getting patients to go to the review sites for you.

The same goes for your emails; your patients may already have an account on one of these review sites and then it would be even easier for them to leave a review saying what a wonderful job you did! This also helps even more since identified reviews count even more than anonymous ones!

Again, it's important to note that these are absolutely, positively not testimonials: these are things consumers can go and do on their own. In fact, you're simply trying to encourage a behavior that's already happening: don't be surprised if, when you start this process, you already have a couple of reviews scattered around the Internet. All you're doing is encouraging this process: you're saying "Hey, there are these review sites out there and having reviews help us. You might do it already, and if you liked our service, your review will really help our Internet ranking and get more people into our door!"

You'll find, more often than not, that people are more than willing to help you out in this regard! They'll go to these sites and fill out reviews, and this is super-important: it's one of the driving forces behind the Google Places / Google + Local rankings, and by having this steady system of reviews you're ensuring your steady climb to the top!

Just the Facts:

- Reviews are very important, and should not be overlooked: search the review sites and find out which ones you should be focusing on.

- Make sure you have a system in place to get users to review you: this is different from testimonials!

- Whatever you do, don't have a computer in your office for patients to write reviews (and absolutely don't write their reviews for them). Google requires the reviews to be written by the client on a computer outside of the office, and so the reviews need to be done on the client's own computer!

- Be careful about who you hire to do your review marketing: some marketers will promise huge numbers but write fake reviews with duplicate content and severely damage your Google ranking!

Chapter 8: **Automation (aka How to Get Robots to Do Your Work for You)**

Follow-up strategies are a vital segment of any Internet marketing strategy, and it's equally vital that you automate it as much as possible; many businesses will try to do this manually, but the overhead required to manually implement isn't feasible for most businesses. It's vital that you don't spend manual time fielding emails and responding one by one; we've had clients in the past who literally sent out e-mail newsletters every week by hand. If somebody new came in, they'd get manually added to this email list.

That sort of system may work in the beginning, but it's easy to see that it doesn't scale up well at all; you need an automated method of follow-up that both preserves quality but also scales out well, freeing up resources and keeping your Internet marketing strategy running smoothly and efficiently!

Follow-up Framework

First off, we have to talk about the framework for follow-up: when we're talking about follow-up, we're talking about traffic generated to you.

We're not talking about people that come in through the door necessarily. We're talking about follow-up that happens when the person finds you; you need a follow-up strategy whether or not the contact is initiated by phone, email, or online via the website.

When a new patient gets to your website and chooses to give their name, phone number, and email address, they go into your funnel. Your funnel is the resource you have where you capture your leads and market to them specifically from there. The reason for this is that they've gone through the trouble of giving you this information—they're a "warm lead" and obviously interested, and you have to get to them fast! The whole function of the funnel is to provide you with a resource that enables this sort of rapid response to whatever communication the patient happened to initiate.

The best way to do this is to set up a basic autoresponder system. This system will provide two things to you: it's going to alert you that someone's given you information, and it's going to send them a message immediately. There are a couple of ways to do this, and later on we'll talk about different techniques including texting and direct voicemail.

The most traditional and common autoresponse, however, is an email—that's something they should be getting immediately

There are many autoresponder services out there that provide these types of systems: Constant Contact, A Weber, Infusion Soft, etc.

Whichever service you go with, you have to make absolutely sure that they have a system in place capable of capturing names, storing names in an organized way, and making it as easy and automated as possible to send out those autoresponders.

You also need to have a strategy in place for phone numbers. If someone gives you their phone number, you should not only email them right away, but also email someone in your office right away a note that says "Hey, this person called interested in this. Here's their number." The reason for this is that the Internet is 24 hours; it doesn't close, it's always open, and your website is happily receiving visitors all around the clock. Your office hours, however, are only during the day; if your office hours are nine to four, for example, you won't be answering phones at ten in the evening.

The reason for emailing your office member is that if somebody comes in at night and submits their information, they get an immediate email; when your person gets in the next morning at nine, they can see the email and know someone tried to get in touch. They can then pick up the phone and say "Hey, this is Bob Jones from Jones, Smith, and Johnson. I saw you downloaded our special report- I hope it helped you out.

I'm just calling to ask if there's anything we can help you with." This is a very personal follow-up to a warm lead, with an emphasis on the personal. We can't stress that enough—you're a local business providing a service to the community and you need to reach out and make those personal connections. The bigger the step, the better; an automated email is the minimum bar to entry. If they've gone through the trouble of giving you their email, you need to say thanks, email back, and throw in a special report; maybe email them again a few days later with another message. These should be automated; you can have a few templates for these emails that you can send out to your warm leads.

It's very important to implement this email / phone call system and use it regularly. This isn't e-commerce, and we're not going to close any deals online; there's no shopping cart, no impulse buy button that's going to magically give you patients without any legwork.

You are still a local business, and we're engaged in local Internet marketing- you can't just send out email and expect things to happen. You need to get that phone call or office visit to seal the deal!

Another good best practice is to email out one of your blog posts per month. Just take one of your blog posts per month, any one of them, and fire it out to anyone on your email lists. It's very easy to send out what's called a "broadcast message" to anyone on your email list still marked as open to receiving communication from you. The reason you want to do this is that, on the whole, this Internet marketing strategy is a long-term strategy; your patients may be thinking they need medical services but they may not need them quite yet. That doesn't mean, however, they won't need them down the line, and these periodic emails will let them remember who you are. This is called "top of mind awareness" in marketing; you want to be on the top of the mind to a patient down the road.

They may one day think "Oh! My dad needs his vision checked for driving purposes. I've been getting these emails from a business down the road who deal with this sort of thing. Maybe I'll give them a call and see if they can answer my questions!"

Just the Facts:

- Follow-up is important, but it's equally important that your follow-up process be automated: no one should be sending out newsletters or follow-ups by hand, nor adding anyone manually to lists.

- Don't just follow-up with your leads when they fill out a form: follow-up in the office as well. This lets an employee call the lead as soon as possible, while they're still warm, and shows the lead that you're friendly and ready to do business.

- It's important to keep regular contact with your patients: fire off a blog post once a month to your email lists, in order to keep your business at the top of their minds.

Chapter 9: **The Bottom Line: ROI and How To Be Sure You Make More Than You Spend**

In typical advertising solutions that we've seen from clients, most of the ad dollars get spent in the Yellow Pages along with some TV and some radio; these make up the vast majority of advertising budgets with clients that we've worked with. They're usually not spending too much money online, and if they are, it's an extension of the Yellow Pages that's usually not well-tracked and often very ineffective.

Advertising online, however, has a huge advantage over traditional advertising methods normally used by most businesses: it's extraordinarily easy to track what's going on throughout the entire online process. You can track pretty well what's happening in each stage of the game: who emailed, what's in the funnel, what's going on, etc. and so forth. This is very difficult to do with regular advertising; quite often, the only method of communication that traditional advertising media gives a client is a phone number.

Unless you're asking them where they heard about you or you're creating a unique phone number for each ad (which is, by the way, a very good best practice; more on that later), you're not getting very good information at all about how your advertising budget is helping you!

In contrast to these traditional advertising methods, you can glean vast amounts of data from the Internet and the tools available to you. You can track how many people visit, and what keywords they typed in that led them to clicking your site. If they visit your Google Places / Google + Local page, you can have instant knowledge there, including who visited, when, and how. Some directory listings have tracking data in place as well; the big Kahuna in this realm, however, is Google Analytics.

Google Analytics is an absolute must-have for your website. If it's not already on your website, ask your webmaster to integrate Google Analytics with your site; if he can't, it's time to find another webmaster. That's how important Google Analytics is to your ROI (Return on Investment). It tells you who's visiting, who's clicking, what data they're entering, how well your website is converting leads, how long your patients stay on your site, and more!

It's an absolutely essential tool for monitoring your ROI and your website, and it needs to be there.

Ok, so once again, you're a Ophthalmologist, right? Not an online marketing geek. While tracking hits and calls is super important (you do need to know where your money is going), we found that most Physicians just don't have the time to do this on a consistent basis. That's why for our private clients, we implemented a system where we track all traffic on their website…and all of the calls to the office. Then at the end of the month, they get a detailed report on all of the action.

We mentioned above having different phone numbers for each ad; even that is more easily tracked online. There are services online that allow you to create different unique forwarding numbers that all forward to your actual number; the only difference is that the call statistics are online and you can easily see at a glance how many calls each number received. This isn't to say you have to get rid of your current phone number—in fact, you shouldn't. These numbers are only forwarding numbers and nothing more; patients with your old number can still get through perfectly fine.

Another great tool is Google Webmaster Tools, specifically because it tells you how many people are linking to you across the Internet and thus how well your Internet marketing strategy is doing overall. This should be complemented by statistics on your email funnel and autoresponders—you should be able to see how many people are getting / opening your emails and keep track of that as well. On top of all that, there's your own internal CRM (Customer Relationship Management system): how much money you're charging, how long you're working, how long you spend with each patient, etc. and so forth. As we'll see, that's an incredibly key resource in determining your ROI.

On that note, we're assuming that you already have an internal CRM in place—it is crucial for this process and others. Discussing the process and tools to manage internal CRM is beyond the scope of this book, and there are many resources available to provide you help and support with implementing your own CRM; it's a vital step in the chain, and you need to have one before you can accurately calculate your

ROI.

There are an almost unlimited number of things you can track online in order to measure your ROI, and if you're going to take anything away from this section it is this: it's imperative that you have a strong, stable, well-defined system in place in order to correctly track your ROI. Most of the clients we work with believe they have a process in place, but when it's subjected to a rigorous examination it turns out that it breaks down. It's a good step that they even have a system in place—it's good sense and a standard marketing practice. They're spending money, and they want to know where that money's going and how that money's helping them. For an Internet marketing strategy, however, you need to go above and beyond: you need to be taking in the data that show you the point of entry for all your patients.

An example monthly run down might look something like this: in total, 155 people visited our site this month. Of those visits, 35 came from Google Places / Google + Local, 120 from Google organic search, and 12 from Facebook fan pages. Of these 155 visits, we followed up with all of them; of the patients we followed up with, we closed 45, and each one of them was worth $1200 on average.

This is very basic, and the numbers are simply example numbers, but it should give you an idea of how you should be looking at and tracking your Internet marketing strategy. This allows you to really get an accurate sense of valuation from patients that find you online: Are they worth the same amount as patients who found you driving by, or from referral? We want to make sure you're capturing ROI information from those patients online, and these are extremely important statistics for you to know. Very often, we end up having to build new systems and processes for clients to get this reporting accurate; make absolutely sure that when planning out your overall Internet marketing strategy, you decide what metrics you're going to use and just how you're going to track them!

We can't stress this point enough: it's vital that you have an understanding of your ROI online all the time. Efficient and accurate monitoring in this realm gives you an unparalleled advantage over traditional media; you can know down to the dollar whether spending in the online arena is good for your ROI. In fact, we tell most of our clients that if they're not getting at least three times their ROI on their Internet marketing that something is really wrong. Usually, it's more than that; three times the ROI is our bare minimum for patients to see. If you're not getting that, it means something's wrong and you need to go back and look again at your strategy. Either you've missed something along the way, or you're in a really competitive market and you need to bring in a second opinion or another expert to help you break into the market.

Tracking your own ROI also gives you another advantage: should you choose to hire a marketing agency for your Internet marketing, you can tell whether or not the marketing agency is working well or not, and you can know whether you should stick with them or find someone new.

TIP:
If you're working with an agency, you should absolutely require them to provide you with these ROI reports. They can get them, and if they're not giving them to you or claim they're unable to get them there's something seriously wrong; they're either hiding something or they're simply not as good as you thought they were!

Understanding your ROI, understanding your Analytics, using online-only phone numbers; all of these things simply underscore a philosophy that you should always adhere to in your online Internet marketing strategy: use every tool and resource available to you to know where your dollars are going and whether or not your online advertising dollars are really pulling their weight. The more control you have over your information flow and tracking information, the more valuable your online strategy is going to be and, ultimately, the more valuable your business as a whole will become!

Just the Facts:

- ROI tracking on print and TV ads is scarce and ineffectual at best: online ROI tracking offers a wealth of information, and enables you to very precisely track where your money is going and how much of it is coming back.

- It's imperative that you have a strong, stable, well-defined system in place in order to correctly track your ROI. Know where your money is going, know what sites are giving you hits, and know what percentage of leads you're converting, from which sites, and how much you're converting them for on average at the very least!

- If you work with a marketing agency, it's vital that they give you these ROI reports: they can give them, and if they can't or don't want to, something is seriously wrong.

Chapter 10: **Where Do I Go From Here**

If you've reached this chapter, give yourself a pat on the back: you've done more for your online Internet marketing strategy than many local businesses will ever do. You've got a very, very solid foundation for pulling patients in from the web; you're ranked high with a no-nonsense website that calls to action, you're a Facebook and Twitter regular, and you have in place a sophisticated system of follow-ups and ROI tracking that will enable you to pinpoint your highest-profit channels with incredible accuracy.

That's no reason to get complacent, however: the Internet is, by its very nature, a fast-moving target. Internet marketing isn't always going to stay in stasis, and you'll have to work to keep up with it. With that in mind, this chapter is dedicated to what's coming up down the road: things that aren't yet a major player in online marketing, but absolutely will be down the line. These are things that a local business has to think about; new technologies and trends that will have to be incorporated into your marketing strategy in order to keep at the top of your game!

Mobile

We've held this particular topic to the very end, but this is perhaps the most immediate of all the coming challenges for Internet marketing.

Mobile devices are rapidly becoming the primary mode of interaction with the Internet; Mary Meeker of Morgan-Stanley has recently estimated that, given current mobile trends, the number of mobile devices that connect to the Internet will eclipse that of regular desktop PCs and laptops by mid-2013. You heard that right: by 2014, more people will be connecting to the Internet by phone than by computer.

In fact, mobile is already a driving force behind many of the search engine changes we've seen. Google is setting up its local places infrastructure because it believes information is going mobile.

Mobile search is a different creature than traditional search; it's more often an immediate need. Users who search mobile are typically driven by an "I need something right now that's near me" mentality, as opposed to a more research-oriented desktop user who's more willing to sift through answers and Wikipedia articles. Very few people will be doing that on a mobile phone; most likely they're looking for a business nearby they can walk or drive to quickly.

This is great news, even for an Ophthalmologist although many clinics have looked skeptically at us when we've said this. Very often, people are out at lunch, driving around, or talking about stuff and think of their problem. More and more, they'll just think to themselves "Oh! I'll just use my phone really quick and search for an answer". The same applies to sitting around eating dinner or watching TV; chances are they have their iPhone, Android phone, or tablet sitting right next to them. Instead of waiting and looking up the answer to their problem later, they'll just pick up their mobile device and look up the answer right then and there. This might seem far-fetched, but it's actually not: think about your own mobile smartphone use, or the usage patterns you've observed in others. There's a clear aura of instant gratification with any sort of mobile device, and users take advantage of it and get an instant answer. If your site's not mobile-friendly or your Google Places / Google + Local page is non-existent (Google Places / Google + Local is extremely mobile friendly) you're going to get left out in the cold.

The mobile realm also tightens up the ranking requirements quite a bit. On the regular desktop Internet, you've got to be in the top 7 ranking; it'd be nice to be in the top 3 or 4, but 7's the bare minimum. On mobile devices, if you're not top 2 you're not being seen; very few people scroll down on mobile phones, and often they simply tap the first or second result they see. This is important to you because mobile phones offer an unparalleled ease of use; for example, many phones like iPhone and Android offer built-in calling from the web. Users can simply tap a finger on your phone number and the smartphone dials the number automatically, without any need to ever pick up another phone. As mobile devices are more and more common, it's of critical importance that your site is mobile-friendly and sits in that A or B listing on Google's result returns!

Social

We've obviously covered a great deal of social media previously, and you're well-equipped to handle the social network scene at the moment. What we didn't cover, however, is the future of social networks- how they're going to change and how that's going to impact your overall online marketing strategy.

The first and most important aspect of future social is this: eventually, social media services are going to be more than just places where people connect. In the future, social media networks are going to transform into something more search engine oriented; people will go to Facebook not just to interact, but to search for things as well. This makes it crucial that you have an established presence early on. It is not too late, and you are not behind the curve: start now having presences on sites like LinkedIn, Twitter, Facebook, YouTube, StumbleUpon, Digg, and other social media sites. This doesn't mean you have to interact with all of these social media network every day or even frequently, though you're going to want to keep more in touch with the big ones as per the social network chapter. What you do want, however, is a presence; just make sure that your listings are in fact on these websites- you'll be very glad for it later!

Social networks are also getting very location-oriented as time goes on, so we can expect that trend to continue: this will eventually lead to a sort of social-mobile combo: users who are Google searching while also in their Facebook mobile app. This is already a user pattern that exists, and we've noticed a rise in this user behavior recently; it's actually quite common now. Users are in the Facebook app and just go to the places listing and see what's around them. The first reaction is that this makes the most sense for restaurants and bars, and they've already start to capitalize on that, but this is useful for businesses as well: users will note "oh, this is where so-and-so office is" and they'll remember it. You need to have this local presence, because if you're not there and you're not found, someone else will be!

This social / search hybrid that we're seeing slowly creep up will also form another important piece of Internet marketing going forward: a combination of social word-of-mouth and Google ranking. Instead of letting Google figure out who's first, more people are going to go on Facebook and see what their friends think. Your interaction level, reviews, and presence on Facebook are going to be crucial at this stage of the game: more people are going to search there the way they're currently searching on Google. Some Internet results will still trickle through, but for the most part the results will come from the patient's social networks.

This is important because people in general will take how their friends and family have viewed businesses very, very seriously: from a marketing perspective, it's a long-known and oft-proven fact that people give far more weight to opinions from friends and family than from any other source of marketing. As a result, this combo of social search is going to be very influential, and you should keep an eye on it and stay on top of it as it progresses.

Direct Mailing to Online Source

You may wonder why we're putting direct mailing in the "What's Next" category; in Internet marketing terms, direct mailing is older than dust.

The reason it's here is that there's definite potential for it as the years roll on: like fashion from the seventies coming back around and becoming popular again, direct mailing is making a comeback. The reason for this is partly because of its scarcity. Receiving mail every now and then, done properly, is not a poor marketing option. It's not something you should rely on heavily, but it's definitely something to keep in your arsenal and use where it's appropriate.

If you already have a direct mail campaign going and want to keep doing it, you need to find a way to incorporate Google Places / Google + Local, Facebook, your website, or a call to action in your direct mailers; you have to shift the goal to getting people online.

Direct mailing with mobile is an especially attractive option; being able to snap a picture and go straight to a website to see info or reviews or being able to text a certain number to get a special report are options that look very promising.

Texting

As mentioned with direct mailing, you can now have people text a number to receive information; they're actually entering your marketing funnel the moment they text that number. This is all automatic, too; you can have the same autoresponder system set up so that it sends texts in the same way that it sends emails. If a user puts in their mobile phone number, they get a text that says something like "We've received your name and email. Thank you very much for getting in contact! Check your email for a special report, free of charge. One of our representatives will be in touch!"

There is one other aspect about texting that should be mentioned here: some in the restaurant / bar type business have automatic texts that send the latest coupons or deals- Tuesday happy hours, Five for Four Fridays, marketing ploys like that. It's very common in the restaurant / bar scene, but we've only started to implement some of those ideas with our clients; truth be told, we're not sure if it will be taken as spammy or not. Depending on your niche, this might work for you.

Once they give out their mobile phone number, don't be afraid to send out texts once or twice a month. Make sure the texts are useful, and don't send them more than once or twice per month; that could start to feel spammy for them. Texts are read over 90% of the time once received as opposed to emails, which are read only 17-20% of the time (and those are optimistic numbers). A well-placed, well-timed text or two every now and then can really help drum up some business and get some patients to call you!

Direct Voicemail

Direct voicemail is the practice of sending a voicemail directly to the phone without the phone ever ringing; this is possible to do now with mobile phone voicemail systems, and in actuality it works very well. These systems are quite nifty; you can set up outbound voicemails that talk about something new or something local that you and your business did. The voicemail can be about thirty to ninety seconds, and instead of calling you can send it directly to their phone. The voicemail notifier pops up but the phone never rings, meaning the client can see the voicemail message and listen whenever they want. It's non-intrusive and as a result the listen rate is much higher.

This is one of the reasons we recommended earlier to get mobile phone numbers from your leads; it not only opens up the texting avenue but the direct voicemail avenue as well. The direct voicemail is very personal and very effective, and it's best used for events or other local things your clinic might be doing. An example might be seminars- if your clinic does seminars in the area about your topic, dropping a direct voicemail to each of your patients is a great, personal way to let them know about your upcoming seminars. It's easy, non-intrusive, and works very well!

Summing Up

We called this chapter the "What's Next" chapter for a reason; many of these technologies are going to or are already beginning to affect the Internet marketing arena. In fact, some of these ideas and strategies that we've talked about are already coming into play. We've begun to experiment with these things with some of our clients who are ahead of the curve or are battling in very competitive markets, which illustrates that these ideas are not simply theory or fluff. They're real strategies that are beginning to come into the market, and it's a good idea to keep abreast of them going forward.

Talk to an agency that you're working with and see what their ideas are on these future strategies. Nothing's set in stone with them, and a creative idea or two could really put you ahead in these arenas. It's also important that you find the right agency, one who specializes in these techniques; these aren't things your average webmaster will know how to do, and chances are an average webmaster hasn't even heard of them! Make sure you talk to an agency or service that thoroughly understands the full realm of Internet marketing, how it works with other marketing, and knowledge of future strategies down the line.

For more help, make an appointment at, **https://www.timetrade.com/book/WSD2Q**

Just the Facts:

- Mobile and social media are going to be the driving forces in marketing over the next few years: both are driving marketing to be more location-oriented, due to the always-on nature that combines and unites mobile and social. Keep up to date on them and don't miss any opportunities to be creative and capitalize on these markets!

- People give much stronger weight to opinions from friends: make sure you have a strong social presence, and leverage that social presence by having a well-established clinic that will rank high in the inevitable search / social hybrid arena.

- Direct mailing still has a place in the world, but it should be driving patients to go to your website in order to get that warm lead and—more importantly—get them to use a channel that's more easily tracked and analyzed.

- Don't ever be complacent: always think of new ways to innovate and incorporate new technologies, and make sure to work with agencies who have a good feel for the online field, are specialists in the online marketing world, and know how to help you stay at the top of your game.

Chapter 11: **How to Get Help Getting All of This Done**

How to Find People to do this for you? The last thing you're going to need is a workforce. Let's face it, you didn't go to school, and build your practice just so you could spend 11 non-billable hours a day uploading videos, submitting listings to directories, and designing websites.

Now we really wish we had better news for you, but finding competent people to do this work for you is not easy. Most web designers are broke, they know nothing about marketing, and many don't have any clients outside of your local city, and yes, they often live in their parent's basement. This is not the kind of person you can trust with your marketing budget so be thorough in deciding who to invest with.

We get asked all the time where to find a good web person. And our answer is that every time we find one who knows what they are doing (they are rare), we hire them to work on our team.

Outsourcing this work to India or to some fly-by-night business will cause more work than it will save.

And having one of your clerks or assistants do this work will drive you both crazy and possibly irreversibly ruin your working relationship.

So How Can I Get All Of This Done?

First, by now you'll agree, local web marketing is probably the most time-sensitive, urgent issue on your clinic calendar right now. It doesn't seem like it at the moment, but when you look back on this book 6-18 months from now, you will probably wish that you had a time machine to get you back to this day.

The local Internet marketing door is WIDE open right now, but it is closing fast…and we would not want you to miss out on securing the financial future of your practice just because you had a big case load.

On the other hand, it's very difficult to find good people to help you with your online presence. Most web designers are flakes. And even if they knew how to put up a good site, it doesn't mean they can get you on page #1 of Google multiple times. And outsourcing this kind of work to India or the Philippines is a waste of time and money. (We've tried it…and won't make that mistake again).

We would love to offer the services of our marketing agency, but at the time of this writing, we are very full with our current paying clients…and our commitment is to them.

In the interest of full disclosure, we provide a turn-key, 100% Done-For-You service which means you send us your business contact information and we do the rest. It's literally ALL done for you. Plus, we know how to get results faster than anyone. Our services are very expensive, and you will probably be able to find someone to do a bare-bones job for much less. But the way to look at it is: we invest a lot of money into our client's future. And, when you get 3, 5, or 9 more patients a month with a life-time value of $4,000.00 or more, we all win.

But we're restricting ourselves to only a handful of clients in any given geographical area. Your area may already be spoken for…and while that's not to say we won't take you, there's a good chance we will be committed already and have to pass.

Having said all of that, if you feel that you are a business that we should choose to work with and you would like to find out about my team's availability to help you and to get all of this DONE FOR YOU, please contact us at…

Phone: 731-332-2350
Email: gfournier@bellsouth.net
Web: **www.FournierMarketingPlan.com**

We will, at the very least, be able to tell you if we are already working with a Ophthalmologist in your area.

If we decide to move forward with you, we always start with a Web Strategy Diagnosis. There is no obligation on either your or our part. This just begins the discussion as to how we may be able to help you. Schedule here: **https://www.timetrade.com/book/WSD2Q**

And while we know that some people take this experience-backed, high-quality web strategy then go and hire a cheap local marketing agency, we also know that the best clients, those who understand the value of growing their clinic by maximizing their online marketing investment will ask us to just "do it for me." We are looking for a small number of clients to build a long-term relationship with. And if that sounds like your clinic, then please feel free to write or call.

With that, we bid you adieu. If you've reached the end of this book, but you certainly haven't reached the end of how we can help you. If you've followed all the techniques and processes in this book and really took it to heart, you're very prepared to wade into the online marketing arena and come out the victor; you're ahead of most of your competitors and you have a clear idea of what lies in store. Don't get complacent, be creative, and you'll be successful in the online marketing arena for many years to come!

Not all the strategies mentioned in this book need to be implemented. There are a variety of options that can build your practice in a very cost-effective manner.

Call Glenn: 6 AM to 2 PM Central Time at 731-332-2350

APPENDIX A: GLOSSARY

ANALYTICS: Analytics are technical measures you can take to see what happens with visitors on your website: how long they stay, what they click, how many of them return to the website, and statistics of that nature. One of the best analytic software packages out there currently is Google Analytics, which is also free.

AUTORESPONDER: An autoresponder is a system put in place to automatically respond to communication initiated by a potential patient, usually via email. Autoresponders can range from simple to extremely complex, and can either send just one generic email or choose from dozens of templates depending on the form used by the potential patient or the information provided to the autoresponder by the potential patient.

BING: A major search engine, like Google and Yahoo. It has many of the same features and has the next-largest market share of any of the search engines, after Google.

BLOG: Originally an abbreviation of the term "web log", it has now come to mean a type of website (or part of a website) that is frequently updated with new content and has many interactive options for users to leave comments and otherwise participate; many blogs are powered by software explicitly designed to make this frequent updating an easier and smoother process, like Wordpress or Typepad.

CALL TO ACTION: Content on a website or other method of communication that appeals to the reader to contact the business.

CONTENT: "Content is King"! Why? Because Google demanded it when they came on the scene 10 years ago. Content has morphed over time and it has been refine to New, Original, Relevant Content.

CRM: An acronym for "Customer Relationship Management". In the context of Internet marketing, it most often refers to the software put in place that manages patients and potential patients of the business;

names, locations, likes, dislikes, needs, and other information that the business may find relevant.

DIRECTORY: In the sense of Internet marketing, a website or part of a website whose purpose is to list businesses. Many of these, like Yelp, Merchant Circle, or CitySearch, also contain reviews of businesses that are often user-generated and submitted.

DUPLICATE CONTENT: Identical content that appears on multiple websites. Search engines have created ways of detecting this and often have algorithms that even detect if the content has just been altered slightly; content that has just be altered slightly and is still virtually identical to the original content will still be flagged as duplicate content by many search engines.

E-COMMERCE: The buying and selling of products and services over the Internet.

FACEBOOK: A social networking site that is currently the most popular in the world; it allows users to network with each other and socialize, including sharing photos, thoughts, status updates, and wall posts with each other.

FACEBOOK PLACES: A specific segment of the social networking site Facebook that allows users to see local spots around them as well as update their location in real-time from mobile phones or other means, allowing other users to see where they are at any given time.

GEOLOCATION: In Internet marketing and SEO, a term used to describe location-specific information; normally city and state for most local businesses.

GOOGLE MAPS: A part of Google's website that primarily deals with maps and navigation. One of the features of Google Maps is the ability for local businesses to list themselves on it, and the local search return feature was originally a part of this system. Google later integrated it into the main search system when it proved to be popular.

GOOGLE PLACES / GOOGLE + LOCAL: A part of Google's website that allows a business to have a specific page dedicated to them. It often hooks in with their location on Google Maps, and it features user-generated reviews of the business as well as links to other directories and review sites.

IP ADDRESS: A unique number that identifies a computer on a network.

KEYWORD: A term that user searches against in a search engine to retrieve content that contains or is relevant to the term.

KEYWORD DENSITY: The use of a specific keyword present in any given piece of content. For example, given the keyword "racing" used five times in a 500-word blog post, the keyword density of "racing" would be 1%. Optimal keyword density is between 3 and 4%, and should not exceed 4% or it may be flagged as spamming.

KEYWORD PHRASE / LONG TAIL KEYWORD PHRASE: A phrase comprised of individual words but treated like a single keyword for the purposes of a search, like "Nascar car racing" or "racing opportunities in Texas".

KEYWORD RICH: Content that has many keywords and uses them often, with good keyword density.

KEYWORD TOOL: Tools created to help select optimal keywords for search engine marketing, like Google's Keyword Tool. They often contain information such as amount of searches for a particular keyword and other metrics that help ascertain how popular or prevalent a given keyword or keyword phrase may be.

LINKEDIN: A social networking site that is geared towards businesses and professionals, enabling them to link up and network more effectively.

LOCAL SEARCH RETURN: A feature within Google's search engine that returns location-specific results for a user who types in keywords that relate to local businesses. For example, a local search return would appear for a user in Omaha, Nebraska who typed in "elder care." A map and local businesses that are relevant to the search result would appear in the ensuing search page.

NICHING: The practice of specializing your marketing strategy to a certain keyword or keyword phrase in order to rank in the highest spot in a local search return for that keyword or keyword phrase.

ROI: An acronym for "Return on Investment," which means the amount of profit; in literal terms, the amount of money returned for the amount of money invested.

SEARCH ALGORITHM: A series of computer algorithms used by major search engines to index, search, and rank websites on the Internet.

SEARCH ENGINE: A website or company, like Google, Bing, or Yahoo, that indexes other websites on the Internet and allows users to enter keywords in order to find relevant websites.

SEO: An acronym for "Search Engine Optimization." It refers to the section of marketing that tries to increase exposure and clientele by using techniques and strategies to rank high on Internet search engines. Often interchanged with SEM (Search Engine Marketing).

SOCIAL MEDIA: Sites whose primary purpose is to enable users to share content with each other and socialize on the Internet; examples of websites that fall into this category are Facebook, Twitter, and LinkedIn.

SPAM: In Internet parlance, spam was originally used to refer to any unsolicited bulk messages sent over email. It is now also commonly used to refer to content on the Internet which is not useful and designed to make a page rank higher on search engines by tricking search engine algorithms into rating the content as more useful than it actually is.

TWEET: An individual post on Twitter.

TWITTER: A social networking service that allows users to post 140-character tweets to their account, with the ability for other users to follow them and respond to the tweets.

UNIQUE SELLING POSITION (USP): Unique Selling Position separates you from your competition in a specific market place. The term is often used to refer to any aspect of an object that differentiates it from similar objects.

URL: An acronym for "Uniform Resource Locator". It is the name that the user types into the browser bar in order to access a specific website; for example, "www.google.com" or "www.bing.com" would be examples of URLs.

END GLOSSARY

About the Author

Glenn started his career as a Consultant Product Designer with companies big and small for about 18 years. Glenn's most interesting assignment was at American Optical. He was thrust into their "Think Tank" with a German inventor and a master machinist to design a Monocular Indirect Recording Ophthalmoscope! Not knowing anything about optics, he spent two weeks absorbing information from their extensive library to design the MIRO.

In the late 1980's computer aided design (CAD) was the thing. At the time there wasn't a standard system being used; each company had their own program which made it impossible for a consultant to get work because of the learning curve. Computers put him out of work!

Then it happened! Glenn was introduced to a new product that blew him away with its simplicity and effectiveness.

He started a new business known as Streak-Free.net without a clue how to market it. Computers put him out of business and it was time for them to get Glenn back in business, so he bought a computer. Now the fun begins.

Glenn had to decide to pay for "Advertising" or invest in himself to learn "Marketing". He invested and has been a student and implementer of Internet Marketing ever since.

StreakFreePro.com had been #1 on Google for 11 years running. We got bumped a little from the last algorithm change, "Hummingbird", competing against 70 to 80 million websites for that top spot!